I have known Eddie Estep for m blessed me not only by the qualit Moses but also especially by the t. The leadership lessons of the life of Moses are extraordinarily relevant for our time.

Gustavo Crocker
General Superintendent
Church of the Nazarene

Combining deep biblical insight and a life of experience in leading others, Estep has again produced a valuable tool for anyone called to lead. In *What's in Your Hand?* Estep again uses both the successes and failures of a biblical leader to provide practical advice for today's leaders, continuing his established practice of frankly describing the real sacrifices required of an effective leader while transparently sharing the joy that comes with making those sacrifices. Using the long and varied life of Moses as a guide, Estep reminds us that leading is a tough, demanding, and sometimes frustrating way life for those who are fortunate enough to be called to the task.

Joseph McLamb
Retired Military Officer/Combat Veteran

If you are asked to lead somebody or something at some point in time, take this book with you. The lessons here will help you arrive at your desired destination, and the folks you bring with you will enjoy the trip.

Bob Broadbooks
Regional Director, USA/Canada
Church of the Nazarene

What's In Your Hand? is a powerful reminder that the God of Moses still asks this penetrating question to those he calls to leadership today. Estep reminds us once again that God's power and his ultimate purpose for our lives are revealed by our response.

David J. Spittal
President
MidAmerica Nazarene University

There are literally thousands of books on leadership. Why not read one based on spiritual truth and time-tested principles? Estep does a masterful job examining the life and leadership of Moses. The beauty of this book is the skillful way unchanging truth is translated to everyday application for the current leader. If you are looking for sound wisdom, leadership development, and practical tips to guide your journey, *What's in Your Hand?* is a book you should read.

Dan Rexroth, Ed.D.
President and CEO
John Knox Village

The exodus from Egypt is arguably the most defining event in the history of the Israelites. The forty-year journey through the wilderness shaped them. God called Moses to lead them. Estep leads us through this amazing journey, gleaning leadership principles from the life of Moses along the way. You will feel like you have followed a master harvester who has picked the grapes off every vine. *What's in Your Hand?* will bless and challenge pastors and lay leaders alike.

Scott Rainey
Global Director of Sunday School and Discipleship Ministries
Church of the Nazarene

Sometimes when you read a book, you hear a person. I think I heard two people in *What's in Your Hand?* I heard Moses reflecting on his frail humanity as he was caught up in the intent of God to liberate a people. And I heard the biblical wisdom of my friend Eddie Estep, who embodies what he writes in these pages. This should give us all hope that we can be shaped by Scripture.

Dan Boone
President
Trevecca Nazarene University

Estep's insightful inquiry, rich research, and artful analysis into one of the greatest leaders in history make *What's in Your Hand?* an essential read for leadership development.

Stanley W. Reeder
Founder, Reeder's Resources

Consultant, Vibrant Church Renewal Estep provides Christendom with a practical review of Moses's life. I could not put down the book! The author interweaves biblical theology narration with godly leadership principles. The book presents practical, day-to-day leadership issues that reflect Estep's experience as a leader. This text is a teaching tool for the servants God is calling to lead.

Christian D. Sarmiento, Ed.D.
Regional Director, South America
Church of the Nazarene

One of the weaknesses of leadership literature is that it often points back to the exploits of the author. Estep, though a gifted leader, instead grounds his work in the life of one of Scripture's most exemplary figures. This book not only distills principles that are timely and effective but also takes the reader through the comprehensive narrative of the life of Moses. It is thoroughly researched, clearly articulated, and eminently practical. *What's in Your Hand?* will be a gift to pastors, small groups or classes, Christian businesses, and leaders of every stripe.

Samuel S. Barber
Lead Pastor
Lenexa (KS) Central Church of the Nazarene

Having read many leadership books that caused me to feel like an aberration, it was refreshing to happily resonate with so many insights in this one. The daring midwives, Shiphrah and Puah, demonstrate that resistance and civil disobedience are sometimes called for in leadership. The unlikely choice of Moses, and not Aaron, is a reminder that God calls needed voices to the work. The assignments given to artists Bezalel and Oholiab show the importance of opening space for creative expression in leadership. These and many more practical and powerful insights make *What's in Your Hand?* an instructive read.

Rev. Vicki Copp, DMin
Lead Pastor
Cameron (MO) Church of the Nazarene

Inspiring and motivational, *What's in Your Hand?* is a must-read for anyone leading through a desert-like season of disappointment or difficulty. Estep is insightful and encouraging in giving practical actions that leaders can take to lead well through whatever challenge they find themselves facing.

Dale Schaeffer
Church Planter and Revitalizer, Florida District Superintendent
Church of the Nazarene

What's in Your Hand? is a must-read for all leaders. Estep has written with biblical authority a spellbinding, captivating, and thought-provoking book about the exciting subject of servant leadership for the newcomer and veteran alike. Estep invites us to take a cross-cultural journey with Moses and the people of God to experience the presence, greatness, and wonders of the Lord.

Carlos Fernandez
Director, Spanish School of Ministry
Kansas City District, Church of the Nazarene

WHAT'S IN YOUR HAND?
LEADERSHIP LESSONS FROM
THE LIFE OF MOSES

EDDIE ESTEP

THE FOUNDRY
PUBLISHING

Cover Design: Merit Alcala
Interior Design: Sharon Page

Library of Congress Cataloging-in-Publication Data
Names: Estep, Eddie, author.
Title: What's in your hand? / by Eddie Estep.
Description: Kansas City : Beacon Hill Press of Kansas City, 2020. | Includes bibliographical references. | Summary:
    "This book follows Moses's challenging journey, offering important leadership lessons on hearing God's voice,
    leading through change, activating your leadership team and more"— Provided by publisher.
Identifiers: LCCN 2020029828 (print) | LCCN 2020029829 (ebook) | ISBN 9780834139503 (paperback) | ISBN
    9780834139510 (ebook)
Subjects: LCSH: Leadership—Biblical teaching. | Moses (Biblical leader)—Biblical teaching. | Leadership—Religious
    aspects—Christianity.
Classification: LCC BS680.L4 E78 2020 (print) | LCC BS680.L4 (ebook) | DDC 248.4—dc23
LC record available at https://lccn.loc.gov/2020029828
LC ebook record available at https://lccn.loc.gov/2020029829.

The Internet addresses, email addresses, and phone numbers in this book are accurate at the time of publication. They are provided as a resource. The Foundry
Publishing does not endorse them or vouch for their content or permanence.

10 9 8 7 6 5 4 3 2

For Diane. The wisdom, joy, and beauty that mark your life produce a sweet perfume that reminds others of Jesus. Accompanying you on life's journey is a gift.

CONTENTS

ACKNOWLEDGMENTS

My deep gratitude is expressed to those whose significant contributions have made this book possible.

Special thanks to Mark Brown, Bonnie Perry, Rene McFarland, Elizabeth Kueffer, Audra Spiven, and all the great people at The Foundry Publishing for their help and encouragement, and for the opportunity to partner in the development of leaders for the church.

I want to thank the following individuals for reading the manuscript and offering numerous and valuable suggestions: Kim Duey, Diane Estep, Scott Estep, Steve Estep, Geoff Kunselman, Greg Mason, and Wayne Nelson. If the book is helpful in any way, it is largely due to their contributions. Where the book falls short, I am solely responsible.

Finally, to the Kansas City District of the Church of the Nazarene, especially the pastors: thank you for the privilege of serving you as I endeavor to put into practice the leadership lessons in this book.

INTRODUCTION
By faith Moses . . .
Hebrews 11:24

The story of Moses, like the stories of all great leaders, revolves around people, places, and events. For Moses, the people he encounters (like Aaron, Pharaoh, and Joshua), the places he visits (like the Egyptian palace, Sinai, and the Red Sea), and the events he experiences (like the burning bush, the plagues, and the giving of the Law) all shape him in significant ways. His story cannot be told without them, nor theirs without him.

If you are a person with leadership responsibilities, there is much to be learned about leadership from the life of Moses. One thing to be learned is that leadership is hard. Period. If Moses, one of the best leaders in history, found leadership to be challenging, you and I should expect no less. Presidential historian Doris Kearns Goodwin identifies one trait as consistent among great leaders: "the ability to transcend both public and private adversity."[1] Moses will face adversity from within his own camp as well as without, yet he remains resolute and purposeful in his leadership. Goodwin concludes, "The leader must be ready and able to meet the challenges presented by the times."[2] Moses, with God's help, will endure the trials and tests presented by the people, places, and events that mark his leadership. Despite many frustrations and human frailties, Moses does not back down or quit but instead grows closer to the heart of God, learning the importance of obedience, patience, courage, faith, and prayer.

Another thing to be learned from Moses is that great leaders spend significant time with God. Moses is unique in the Old Testament. He sees and speaks with God in a distinct manner. He is unique among his contemporaries and successors. Deuteronomy notes, "Since then, no prophet has risen in Israel like Moses, whom the LORD knew face to face" (34:10). This sentiment also appears in Exodus: "The LORD used to speak to Moses face to face, as a man speaks to his friend" (33:11, ESV). The degree of intimacy and immediacy with which Moses sees and speaks with God is exceptional, and his example of intercessory prayer is noteworthy. He is able to instinctively turn to God in prayer when facing significant challenges.

So how does Moses do it? How is he the greatest spokesperson for God as well as the greatest worker of miracles in the Old Testament? How does he become one of the greatest leaders in the Bible? What is his secret? *He spends significant time with God.*

Lastly, we can also learn from Moses that God chooses inadequate people in order to show *God's* power and adequacy. D. L. Moody describes Moses's life in these stages: "Moses spent his first forty years thinking he was somebody. He spent his second forty years learning he was a nobody. He spent his third forty years discovering what God can do with a nobody."[3]

Moses's burial site is neither known nor marked. But if Moses had a monument or a gravestone, there are several potential epitaphs that could be put on it, including:

"Friend of God" (Exodus 33:11)

"Mighty in Word and Deed" (Acts 7:22)

"By Faith" (Hebrews 11:24)

Like Moses, may the people, places, and events that you and I encounter in leadership provide opportunities for us to be good, godly leaders.

— ONE —

EGYPT: WHEN DETOURS BECOME DESTINATIONS

*Your descendants will be strangers
in a country not their own . . .*
Genesis 15:13

To receive this first lesson on leadership, we have to look back to Egypt just before the time of Moses. For several centuries, ancient Egypt was the preeminent civilization in the Mediterranean world. Located in North Africa on the Mediterranean Sea, Egypt was home to one of the oldest civilizations on earth. The heart of Egypt—physically, economically, socially, and religiously—was the Nile River, which flowed through the center of the land, making it lush with rich, dark soil. As the source of Egypt's economic wealth, the river created a natural highway as well as a fertile region. The Nile will play a significant role in the story of Moses.

The history of the Hebrews in Egypt begins with the account of Joseph. Joseph's brothers grow jealous over his dreams and his favored status with their father, and they plan to kill him by throwing him into a pit. They then hatch a plot to sell Joseph to Midianite traders who take Joseph to Egypt, where he is sold to

Potiphar. After being falsely accused of assault by Potiphar's wife, Joseph is thrown into prison, where he gains a reputation as an interpreter of dreams.

When Pharaoh suffers from a troubling dream that none of his advisors can interpret, Joseph is summoned from prison. He interprets Pharaoh's dream and is made second in command over all Egypt. Sometime later, Jacob sends his sons to Egypt to find food when famine strikes their part of the world. Joseph has seen to it that Egypt is not only prepared for the famine but also has enough grain in supply to sell to neighboring countries. When Jacob's sons appear before their brother to buy food, Joseph is made known to them and summons all of them, including his father, to Egypt, where they can be sustained during the famine.

When the Hebrews first come to Egypt, they are treated well because of Joseph. Joseph has been used by God to deliver the Egyptians in a time of great famine, and Pharaoh has favored him and his people. With the approval of Pharaoh, the Hebrews settle in Goshen, a land well suited for their flocks and herds.

In the beginning, Egypt is a place of blessing. In the end, Egypt is a place of oppressive burden. While God uses Egypt to save Israel from famine and extinction, in time Egypt will become a place of bondage and misery for the Hebrews. Their place of sanctuary and security will become a place of affliction and slavery.

But Egypt is never intended to be the permanent home of God's children—not for Joseph of the Old Testament and his family, nor for Joseph of the New Testament and his family. Egypt is never intended to be the final destination, though God's children do, by necessity, sometimes find themselves as sojourners in a land that is not their home.

When Israel finally leaves Egypt, they show their propensity for making destinations of detours. God sends them on a detour at the beginning of the Exodus, intentionally taking them on a roundabout route to Canaan because the more direct route will mean war. But what was meant to be a detour will become a destination for an entire generation who passes away in the wilderness because of their disobedience.

Leadership Lesson: Detours are often part of the journey, but they are rarely intended to be the final destination.

With God's help, you can choose what becomes your permanent address.

Some of the places of disappointment or hurt you encounter in your life, God intends to be temporary, or seasonal. The temptation is to settle in those places of discontentment or frustration and to allow them, over time, to become places of bitterness or resentment. This happens often in the wilderness wanderings of the Israelites. One of the places they set up camp will even be named "Bitterness."

In time, even a place that was originally one of refuge and deliverance from life's storms can become one of tyranny and repression. A place that was once a great blessing can become a place of great burden.

When one of life's detours takes you to Egypt, find a trusted voice to help you process the journey, identify your present situation as a detour, and remind you not to settle there. See your present difficult situation for what it is—a season, not a lifetime; a detour, not a destination. Don't allow yourself to become too comfortable in Egypt. Don't make a detour a destination.

Questions for Leadership Development

1. How do you tell the difference between a detour and a destination?

2. Identify a time in your life when you found yourself on a detour. How did you respond?

3. Would you characterize the present season of your life as a detour or a destination? Why?

— TWO —

PHARAOH, PART 1: FEAR-BASED LEADERSHIP

Then a new king, to whom Joseph
meant nothing, came to power in Egypt.
Exodus 1:8

In Scripture, we learn that "pharaoh" is the title given to the rulers of Egypt, and that it functions much like "king" or "emperor" or "governor." Throughout the Old Testament, there are numerous pharaohs in power. The first time a pharaoh appears in the Bible is in Genesis 12, when Abram's wife, Sarai, catches the eye of the ruler of Egypt. The next appearance, of a different pharaoh, happens in the story of Joseph (see Genesis 37-47), when Joseph is sold to Potiphar, who is one of Pharaoh's officials. After Joseph is wrongly imprisoned, he has an opportunity to interpret Pharaoh's dream. As a result, Joseph gains favor with Pharaoh and is named second in command of the whole nation of Egypt.

When famine strikes the land during Joseph's watch, he invites his family to relocate to Egypt, where the resources needed for life are in sufficient supply. At first, just one Hebrew—Joseph—makes his home in Egypt. But seventy members of his family follow: all those who accompany the Israelite patriarch Jacob into Egypt. As the decades pass, the Israelites begin to multiply. According to Exodus 12:37, the population of the Israelites in Egypt grows to include six hundred thousand men who are capable of bearing arms. When the number of women, children, and elderly are added, we can reasonably assume the total eclipses two million Israelites. The Hebrews increase in number from seventy to more than two million in just four centuries.

Life grows and changes quickly, doesn't it? As Exodus opens, a new pharaoh has come to power in Egypt. Unlike the pharaoh in Joseph's story, this pharaoh is a ruthless, driven leader "to whom Joseph meant nothing" (Acts 7:18).

Leadership Lesson: The loss of community memory can have a significant impact on a group, organization, or institution.

In this example, because Pharaoh does not know the story of Joseph, he has lost a vital link to both his own history and the history of the Hebrew people. The story of intersection between Joseph and Egypt have profound historical implications. Pharaoh's lack of awareness of this story will have intense repercussions.

To lead well, you must know the story of the people you serve. Four centuries after Joseph, the new pharaoh is unaware that God once used a Hebrew to bless Egypt and the surrounding nations. As a result of his unfamiliarity with the story of Joseph, Pharaoh will make decisions that prove catastrophic for Egypt. It is important to know the history—the stories—of the people you lead. Knowing those stories gives you a valuable perspective and understanding that will allow for more informed decision-making.

Leaders always step into (or find their place in) a story that is already being written. You must become familiar with the history of your leadership context.

Egypt's new leader alters the existence of the people of Israel. No longer do they enjoy the good life. Pharaoh, who remembers neither Joseph nor his story, changes their reality. But why?

The Israelites are "exceedingly fruitful; they multiplied greatly, increased in numbers and became so numerous that the land was filled with them" (Exodus 1:7). The growth of the Hebrew population in Egypt does not escape the notice of Pharaoh, who views their increasing numbers as a threat.

Fear becomes the primary motivation of Pharaoh's leadership. His anxiety is threefold. He is afraid that the Hebrews will, by sheer number, overwhelm the Egyptians. He is afraid that the presence of so many Jews will become a security risk (for instance, if there is an outside invasion, the Jews might align themselves with the enemy). And he is afraid the Hebrews will leave, thus eliminating the slaves he needs. Pharaoh's fear provides three corresponding motivations in enslaving the Hebrews: population control, national security, and economic wealth. Pharaoh is afraid of what *might* happen. The Israelites *might* increase more. The Israelites *might* revolt. The Israelites *might* devastate Egypt's economy by leaving the country.

Leadership Lesson: Ruthless leaders often use the excuses of national security and economic stability to rationalize policies that lead to brutality and the oppression of the powerless.

In Pharaoh's case, the policies that lead to economic advantage for Egypt come at the cost of the Israelites' freedom. One can easily observe similar patterns throughout world history. And it's not hard to see how leaders leverage those same fears today.

Pharaoh's fear becomes so great that he takes steps to control the rapid multiplication of the Israelite people. He devises a way that not only will eliminate them as a threat to national security but also will make them an asset to the national economy. Pharaoh settles on a plan to oppress them, hoping to reduce their numbers by forced labor.

The Hebrews, originally shepherds, are now pressed into service in the brick fields. They are forced to provide the labor needed to build two store cities for Pharaoh. Their slave labor provides affordable public works. The Israelites will become the backbone of the Egyptian economy. Pharaoh needs enough of them to produce an ample supply of bricks but not so many that they can rebel. (It's a situation that should feel hauntingly familiar to Americans today, as we remember that the eighteenth- and nineteenth-century slaves in the United States found a strong connection between their plight and the plight of the enslaved Hebrews in Egypt.)

In Egypt, slave masters are put over the Hebrews to ruthlessly oppress them and make their lives bitter with harsh labor. Pharaoh resolves to wear them out and reduce both their numbers and their spirit by the rigor of the work. While fear is behind the oppressive treatment the Israelites receive at the hands of the Egyptians, Pharaoh benefits by lessening their threat to national security and increasing his economic advantage with free slave labor.

Leadership Lesson: Fear-based leadership often leads to oppression.

Fear causes leaders to act in ways that repress the freedom of those they lead. Pharaoh is at the top of the power pyramid. He has everything, yet he grows anxious at what he perceives to be a threat to his kingdom. Perhaps the more a leader has to lose, the easier it is to become anxious and fear-driven.

God calls leaders to bless people rather than oppress them. As a leader, you should evaluate whether your policies tend to result in blessing or oppression, and whether your practices lay burdens on the backs of people or empower them to become better, freer, and more whole.

Do people follow you because they are afraid of you and afraid of the consequences for not following you, or do they follow you because they know you care about them as much as you do the mission? Does your team feel fear, shame, or anxiety as a result of serving with you? Or, do they feel joy, hope, and a sense of purpose and accomplishment as a result of serving with you?[1]

If the people under your care are in bondage, you need to reevaluate your leadership practices.

Slavery is Pharaoh's first solution to what he views as the problem of Israel's population explosion. He hopes forced labor will deplete their numbers, ensuring that they will not have the time or the energy to reproduce. That the Israelites experience adversity in Egypt cannot be denied. They are made slaves, they are overworked, and they are undercompensated. However, Egypt's oppression proves futile and leads to greater increase. The more the Hebrews are oppressed, the more they multiply.

The fruitfulness of the Israelites is a result of God's favor and a reminder of God's initial blessing to humanity in Genesis 1: "Be fruitful and increase in number; fill the earth . . ." (v. 28).

Leadership Lesson: **Leaders do well to remember that adversity is not void of blessing.**

The ruthless, fear-driven Egyptian leader cannot hold back the blessings of God. God's people often testify to the truth of this paradox: the more adversity, the more blessing. The Israelites flourish because of divine blessing. They flourish *in spite of* their circumstances. The same can be seen throughout church history. Persecution has most often resulted in the flourishing of the church, not its diminishment.

In spite of Pharaoh's oppression, the Hebrews continue to multiply. Their fruitfulness only increases Pharaoh's fear, which leads to more ruthless oppression, which leads to more fruitfulness, which leads to even greater atrocities.

Leadership Lesson: **Don't fear what God is blessing.**

Leaders who are not aligned with God may become anxious about what God is blessing when it is perceived as a threat to their own kingdom. Leaders can grow fearful of what God is blessing because of the potential impact on their own power or position. We might perceive the growing prominence of others as a diminishment of our own standing. However, God's blessing and provision will not be thwarted by oppression or a leader's fear-based insecurity.

Fear-based leadership can easily become phobia-based leadership. When Pharaoh's program of oppression fails to stop the population growth of the Hebrews, he gives instructions that all male Hebrew babies be put to death at birth.

Pharaoh's oppression of the Hebrews occurs in two stages. The first stage is slavery; the second stage is genocide. When slavery does not bring about the desired population control, Pharaoh turns to infanticide. He devises a clever strategy for the slaughter of Israel's baby boys and instructs the Hebrew midwives to kill them during the delivery process.

When the midwives ignore Pharaoh's directive and he calls them on it, they give a dubious explanation: "Hebrew women are not like Egyptian women; they are vigorous and give birth before the midwives arrive" (Exodus 1:19). Pharaoh realizes the decree that the midwives dispose of male Hebrew infants is ineffective, so he intensifies the genocide by commanding the Egyptian population at large to carry out the mass murder of the Hebrew babies. The final solution is the murder of all male infants by throwing them into the Nile River.

This may be the first documented example of anti-Semitism in history, but it certainly will not be the last. Pharaoh is only the first in a long line of disastrous leaders whose leadership is marked by death rather than by life. A similar narrative appears in the New Testament. When Herod learns of the birth of Jesus from the wise men, he orders the death of all male children in Bethlehem under the age of two in a desperate attempt to kill the promised child.

Though the Hebrews are multiplying, they are also suffering. And God will notice their suffering. God's people need a deliverer. God will hear the cries of his people and provide a deliverer, but the deliverer will first need to be delivered himself.

Questions for Leadership Development

1. How do leaders become familiar with the stories of the people they lead?

2. In what kinds of situations are you prone to exhibit fear-based leadership? What are you most afraid of?

3. Is it possible for a leader who burdens people to transform into a leader who blesses people? How might that happen?

THREE

SHIPHRAH AND PUAH: CIVIL DISOBEDIENCE

*I became convinced that noncooperation
with evil is as much a moral obligation
as is cooperation with good.*
Martin Luther King, Jr.[1]

Moses's very existence can be attributed to the gracious and courageous actions of six different women. At various times in Moses's life, these women act to bring about his deliverance. The six women are Shiphrah and Puah (the Hebrew midwives), Jochebed (Moses's mother), Miriam (Moses's sister), Pharaoh's daughter, and Zipporah (Moses's wife). Even though Moses is born into a world of genocide, God will use several women to deliver the one who will be used by God to deliver the Israelites.

Pharaoh's fear of a growing population of slaves leads to terrible brutality. He determines to control the growing population of Hebrew slaves by killing their male babies, and he demands the help of the Hebrew midwives to do that.

A midwife is a person who helps women during labor and delivery, and after the birth of their babies. Midwives provide the security of an experienced hand to comfort expectant mothers and help deliver their babies. Their work is especially important in cultures in which obstetricians or hospitals are rare. With so many Hebrew women bearing children, it is likely that Shiphrah and Puah are chief midwives and have other women working under their supervision.

Pharaoh instructs the midwives to watch as Hebrew babies are born. If it is a girl, the birth is to take place naturally. However, if it is a boy, the midwife is to snuff out its life: "When you are helping the Hebrew women during childbirth on the delivery stool, if you see that the baby is a boy, kill him; but if it is a girl, let her live" (Exodus 1:16).

In one of the first recorded acts of civil disobedience in the Bible, Shiphrah and Puah refuse to go along with Pharaoh's plan. They refuse to obey an evil law because of a higher good. These women remind us that just because it's legal doesn't mean it's moral.

Leadership Lesson: Godly leadership may mean assuming the role of resistance and appropriate civil disobedience.

Courageous resistance is called for when those in authority call you to do what you know is wrong. When human laws are contrary to God's laws, then we "must obey God rather than human beings" (Acts 5:29). There are several notable examples of this in the Bible, including Daniel's refusal to obey King Darius's prohibition against prayer in Daniel 6 and the three Hebrew children's refusal to bow a knee to Nebuchadnezzar's image of gold in Daniel 3. There are also examples from more recent history, including the stories of Dietrich Bonhoeffer and Corrie Ten Boom as well as the Civil Rights Movement of the 1940s, 1950s, and 1960s in the United States.

When it comes to civil disobedience, author and theologian Warren Wiersbe says, "When Christians disobey the law because of their conscience, their decisions must be based on the clear law of God found in Scripture, and not simply on personal prejudice. Note too that the midwives, Daniel and his friends, and the apostles were courteous in the way they dealt with the civil authorities."[2]

As people living in a fallen world, there are times when we may have to choose between greater and lesser evils. In such times, we need the wisdom of God to direct us (James 1:5). "As long as this world is in the travail of sin (Rom. 8:22)," Wiersbe warns, "we will face difficult decisions."[3] Old Testament professor H. Junia Pokrifka speaks to the responsibility of godly leaders in our day: "God continues to call people into civil disobedience like that of the Hebrew midwives whenever leaders and their policies oppose God's justice and sanctity of life."[4]

The midwives will deliver Moses twice—once from the womb of Jochebed, and a second time from the threat of Pharaoh. Motivated by their respect for God (Exod. 1:17), they resist Pharaoh's decree and refuse to kill the boys and make it look like a stillbirth. Instead of obeying Pharaoh, they allow the children to live. As a result of their courage, God blesses the midwives and gives them "families of their own" (v. 21). They are rewarded for their godly courage.

Leadership Lesson: **Oftentimes, the best rewards for virtuous service are given by God rather than people. Experiencing the favor of God is to be preferred above any human award or honor.**

When it becomes obvious to Pharaoh that his first decree is not producing the desired results, he asks the midwives to explain themselves. They lie to Pharaoh, telling him that the rugged Israelite mothers give birth before the midwives can get to them. Their wise answer deflects the Egyptian ruler's attention away from the midwives.

Leadership Lesson: The names remembered in history often belong to those whose lives reflect uncommon courage.

It is noteworthy that we know the names of the two heroic Hebrew midwives. Their names are remembered and celebrated. But the name of this particular pharaoh is not remembered in the biblical record of Israelite history.

Pharaoh then issues a second ruling that applies not just to the midwives but to all of Egypt: "Every son who is born you are to cast into the Nile, and every daughter you are to keep alive" (Exod. 1:22, NASB). The first edict—"kill the boys"—is specifically given to the midwives. The second edict—"cast all the boys into the Nile"—is given to all.

It was already a challenge for a Hebrew baby boy to survive childbirth, but it has now become almost impossible.

Questions for Leadership Development

1. Is civil disobedience a viable option for a Christ follower? Why or why not?

2. What are some instances in which stories of civil disobedience have inspired you?

FOUR

JOCHEBED: A BASKET CASE

*By faith Moses' parents hid him for
three months after he was born, because they
saw he was no ordinary child, and they
were not afraid of the king's edict.*
Hebrews 11:23

About the time all of Egypt is commanded to throw Hebrew baby boys into the Nile, a Hebrew woman named Jochebed gives birth to a boy who will become known by the name of Moses. Moses has a death warrant from birth. Pharaoh's decree means that Moses is born into a world in which his life expectancy is zero.

Jochebed is married to Amram. Amram is Moses's father. We are not told much about Moses's parents. We are simply told that they are of the house of Levi, which establishes Moses's priestly pedigree (see Exodus 6:19-20). We do know that Amram and Jochebed have faith because Hebrews 11:23 praises that faith. Amram is not named in Exodus 2 but is listed in Old Testament genealogies in Exodus 6, Numbers 3, and 1 Chronicles 6. Jochebed means "the honor of Jehovah." She is mentioned by name only twice in the Bible, in Exodus 6 and Numbers 26. Amram and

Jochebed have two other children besides Moses: Miriam and Aaron. Aaron is three years older than Moses (Exodus 7:7). We are not told Miriam's age, but we can reasonably estimate from the story in Exodus 2:1-10 that she is probably eight to ten years older than Moses.

From his birth, Moses is seen as extraordinary (Exodus 2:2; Acts 7:20; Hebrews 11:23). There seems to have been something significant about Moses's appearance. Even though every mother thinks her child beautiful, Moses is exceptional. He is such a handsome baby that his parents decline to surrender him to the Nile. Instead, they choose to hide him quietly in seclusion. They are willing to defy Pharaoh and do everything in their power to save Moses.

In this story, we get the sense that a conviction grows in Amram's and Jochebed's hearts regarding the great destiny that awaits their baby. Believing that God has a special purpose for him, they do what they can to keep Moses alive by concealing his existence. This is not easy to do when all Egyptians have become Pharaoh's spies.

Moses is successfully hidden for the first three months of his life, but eventually his parents know they cannot keep him a secret any longer. So Jochebed weaves a papyrus basket and coats it with pitch to make it buoyant and waterproof. Her plan is elegant in its simplicity. Moses will be placed in the little ark and carefully set afloat among the reeds on the banks of the Nile. She is obeying the letter of the law, if not the spirit of it.

The Hebrew word used for the papyrus basket occurs in only one other place in the Bible—as a description for Noah's ark. Jochebed makes a miniature ark to save Moses. Peter Enns, a well-known author and theologian, observes the special connection between Noah and Moses. Both, he says, are selected to undergo a tragic, watery fate, both are placed in an ark, and both are the vehicles through whom God creates a new people. Moses's safe passage through the waters of the Nile looks both backward to the flood story and forward to his eventual passage through the Red Sea.[1]

Jochebed tells her daughter, Miriam, to watch the child as the basket is placed at a location where Pharaoh's daughter is known to bathe. That morning, when the Egyptian princess comes to the Nile to wash, she sees the basket, hears the baby's cries, and is moved to compassion for to him. Miriam, on cue, approaches Pharaoh's daughter and asks if she can be helpful by finding a nurse for the baby.

Leadership Lesson: The faithful actions of parents can be life-giving to children.

Jochebed and Amram have faith to believe that God has special plans for their baby. That faith allows them to take risks and to believe they can act in ways that will protect their baby. "Basket case" is a term that usually refers to someone who has lost the ability to function rationally. In this basket case, however, Jochebed is functioning faithfully, wisely, and cleverly. Her creative actions will save the life of Moses. The prayers and faithful actions of godly parents have contributed much to the kingdom of God.

Moses's parents are great models of seeing and instilling a sense of destiny in a child. It would be a beautiful thing if all parents could see and nurture the God-given gifts and potential in their children.

Jochebed, Moses's mother, is employed by Pharaoh's daughter to be Moses's nurse. In an ironic twist of providence, Jochebed is paid to care for her own son. While nursing is required for physical survival, health, and growth, the bond between Moses and his birth mother provided formation of his identity as a Hebrew rather than as an Egyptian prince.[2]

We do not know how long Moses stayed with his mother. It was probably no longer than three or four years, just until he was weaned. But Moses's mother would have provided him not only with milk but also nurture and instruction. Moses would have undoubtedly learned about his providential deliverance by the hand of God as well as gained a rudimentary understanding of the Hebrew people. Thus, Moses grew up to be comfortable in two worlds—Hebrew and Egyptian—and that knowledge would serve him well in years to come.

Questions for Leadership Development

1. What impact has the faith of your parents had on your life?

2. If you have children, what impact has your faith had on their lives?

— FIVE —

ANGER, PART 1: HITTING PEOPLE

Violence does, in truth, recoil upon the violent,
and the schemer falls into the pit
which he digs for another.
Sir Arthur Conan Doyle[1]

There is a forty-year gap in the story of Moses. The Bible is silent about his experiences as a child, teenager, and young adult in the court of Pharaoh. One verse portrays Moses as a baby, and in the next he is a fully grown man, a prince in Egypt. It appears that Moses is being nurtured for the Egyptian throne and prepared by Pharaoh's daughter for a proper life in Pharaoh's court. The New Testament tells us that "Moses was educated in all the wisdom of the Egyptians and was powerful in speech and action" (Acts 7:22).

The epochs of Moses's life can be divided into thirds: the first third as a prince in Egypt, the second third as a shepherd in Midian, and the last third as a deliverer leading God's people through the wilderness. When Moses is forty years old, he makes what will become a life-altering decision "to visit his own people, the Israelites" (Acts 7:23). We are not told why Moses decided to go. It is possible that his responsibilities necessitated him observing

39

Egyptian-Hebrew relations. Maybe he was drawn to explore his roots. Whatever prompted him, he goes and, while there, he witnesses a tragic scene—a Hebrew being beaten by an Egyptian.

As Moses observes the slave labor, his emotions must be stirred. He then sees an Egyptian taskmaster beating a Hebrew, one of his own people. It is possible that the Egyptian officer is not just disciplining the Hebrew slave but is in fact beating him with intent to kill. One wonders if Moses first identifies with the Egyptian only to find himself moved by a sense of kinship with the slave. The repeated expression "his own people" (Exodus 2:11) indicates that Moses feels an affinity and strong identification with the Israelites.

Leadership Lesson: The ability to identify with those who suffer is a significant component of effective leadership.

God's people are suffering in Egypt. In Exodus 2, Moses begins to identify with that suffering. Part of the development of a leader is the ability to have empathy for others.

The Egyptian's beating of the Israelite slave evokes a strong response in Moses. Stirred by compassion for the oppressed, Moses springs into action. In a sudden outburst of anger, he kills the Egyptian. Here we have the first indication that anger is an issue for Moses. Indeed, his anger will flare up again and again before his story is over. At times Moses is volatile, full of stormy energy. In this case, and in others that follow, Moses will not provide a thoughtful, prayerful response to circumstances but instead a rash, emotion-fueled reaction.

Leadership Lesson: **When leaders have unchecked anger, situations become worse.**

One temptation for a passionate leader is to "move things along" in the flesh. The Biblical directive, "'Not by might, nor by power, but by my Spirit,' says the LORD Almighty" (Zechariah 4:6), is a helpful reminder that leaders serve best when acting in sync with God's ways.

When leaders operate in the flesh, the results are usually less than desirable. Acting on impulse is giving into the temptation of pride—human strength at work. Certainly, violence is not the answer. Deliverance brought about by sinful means is not deliverance at all. Author F. B. Meyer refers to Moses's murder of the Egyptian taskmaster as his "first attempt at deliverance."[2] Moses acts in his own power—rash, impetuous, and headstrong.

It is possible for leaders to believe they are doing the will of God and that they are driven by kingdom purposes but instead are taking matters into their own hands. If so, such leaders will find that God cannot bless their work.

Moses's action is hot-blooded, but it is also premeditated. The Bible states that Moses looks around to make sure there are no witnesses before he strikes the Egyptian (Exodus 2:12). He takes justice into his own hands, ensuring it is an opportune time to act and that he will not be observed by a witness. Moses then slays the Egyptian and buries the body in the sand.

Leadership Lesson: **"Hiding wrong doesn't erase wrong. It only postpones its discovery."[3]**

If you have to cover up your behavior, you can be assured that you haven't acted according to the will of God. Anger, when buried, is always buried alive. And it always comes back to haunt the one who buried it.

——————

Neither Moses's anger nor the Egyptian's corpse will remain hidden for long. Unfortunately for Moses, the Hebrew victim of the Egyptian witnesses the murder, and Moses's action will soon be publicly known.

Moses quickly learns that it is not just the Egyptians who are prone to violent aggression. The next day Moses tries to reconcile two Hebrews who are fighting. They reject his help. Moses, protesting the violence, cries out, "Why are you hitting your fellow Hebrew?" (Exodus 2:13). The aggressor taunts Moses by reminding Moses of his own violence the day before.

Moses is not hailed as a hero. He is betrayed by the very people he has just defended. His secret is out. Filled with apprehension and dread, he knows his life is now in danger. When Pharaoh learns of the murder, he wants Moses's life. It may very well be that Pharaoh never trusted Moses. Perhaps he has been waiting for Moses to slip up or prove himself an enemy of Egypt. When Moses murders the Egyptian, Pharaoh again tries to kill Moses, this time directly (v. 15).

Moses's first act of identification with his people ends in failure. He has murdered an Egyptian and must flee Egypt. In the span of a few verses, Moses goes from being a prince with privileged status to an exiled fugitive in a foreign land.

——————

Leadership Lesson: Leaders are capable of doing the right thing the wrong way.

It is right to defend the powerless and those against whom violence is being committed. That is the right thing to do. However, it is wrong to defend people by inflicting upon their abusers the same violence.

As author James Boice says, "We do not advance our cause by killing Egyptians."[4] As a result of Moses's action, even his own people will reject him. When God-called leaders do their work in worldly ways, the results are neither God-honoring nor community-building. "Spiritual ends are never achieved by carnal means," says Charles Swindoll. "You cannot plant a carnal act and grow spiritual fruit."[5]

When you neglect to seek God's direction, and insist on handling things yourself, you usually end up with a mess on your hands. It is not enough for leaders to do the right thing; they must do the right thing the right way.

Moses has failed, and he has failed in epic fashion. His failure is public, and it has significant consequences. As a result, the trajectory of his life will change.

Leadership Lesson: One failure does not necessarily disqualify you from future service.

All too often, when leaders fail publicly it becomes easy for them to shut down and withdraw, overwhelmed by embarrassment and shame. Such leaders sometimes consider themselves ineligible for future service. Moses certainly fails, but that does not mean that God cannot or will not use him. In spite of his failure, Moses will learn that God has significant plans for his future.

Questions for Leadership Development

1. How would you characterize the role of empathy in your leadership?

2. What are indicators that a leader has anger issues?

3. Can you recall a time when you did the right thing the wrong way?

4. As leaders, how can we ensure we are responding in sync with the Spirit rather than impulsively reacting in human strength?

SIX

MIDIAN: WHERE LEADERS ARE PREPARED

There isn't a single battered leader in the Scriptures who would have opted out of the story simply because it cost so much to be used by God. That's because they all had discovered Paul's surpassing joy. How did they do that? By paying attention to holy drama within their souls, which was the only way they could be of sacred use to the people they were called to serve.

M. Craig Barnes[1]

Before Moses becomes Israel's redeemer, he experiences Israel's rejection and becomes an outcast. When Moses arrives in Midian, he is a fugitive from justice and a man without a country. He sits down wearily by a well. He has outdistanced any Egyptian posse that might be trailing him, and he is ready to rest. At the well he encounters the daughters of the priest of Midian. The shepherdesses are being bullied by shepherds rudely demanding the water the women have drawn. Moses intervenes for the women, the intimidators leave, and the shepherdesses invite Moses home to enjoy the hospitality of their father, Jethro.

Like Isaac and Jacob, Moses meets his future spouse at a well. He ultimately marries one of the shepherdesses, and Jethro provides for Moses both a wife (his daughter Zipporah) and a job herding his sheep.

For Moses, Midian becomes the place of preparation. He will spend the next forty years of his life being a shepherd (see Exodus 7:7; Acts 7:23). The one who would have been prince of Egypt now finds himself alone in the wilderness tending sheep. Warren Wiersbe says, "The man who was 'mighty in word and deed' is now in the lonely pastures taking care of stubborn sheep, but that is just the kind of preparation he needed for leading a nation of stubborn people."[2]

Author and attorney Jonathan Kirsch knocks the shine off any romanticized view of a shepherd's daily work. He explains,

The real work of a shepherd is arduous, dirty, and lonely. The flock must be fed and watered every day, and so every day is an urgent search for a new meadow and a new spring. Curious and sometimes unruly animals must be kept from straying too far from the flock. Jackals, hawks, and other predators must be kept at bay with nothing more than a shepherd's hooked staff. Above all, the shepherd is alone in his work—the flock relies wholly on the shepherd, and the shepherd relies on no one but God. Even a matter-of-fact job description of a shepherd's work, however, fairly rings with larger and grander meanings, both spiritual and political, and the Bible makes the most of them.[3]

Midian is the place where shepherds are made, and where the prince will learn to lead. Midian is the place where God sends Moses to leadership school. His classroom is the wilderness, the place leaders are shaped, forged, and proven. His followers are the sheep under his care. His teacher is God, who has led him to Midian in order to form his character in the solitude of the desert. Moses's character will take years to form, and that happens in the wilderness of Midian.

During the forty years Moses serves as a shepherd, he is also getting in touch with his Hebrew heritage. The Israelite patriarchs were nomads who followed their herds and flocks around Canaan. When Jacob and his twelve sons settled in Egypt as a result of famine, Joseph's brothers told Pharaoh that their family was knowledgeable in caring for herds and flocks (Genesis 47:3). Moses is now experiencing the lifestyle and learning the lessons that his people have been experiencing and learning for centuries.

We don't know Moses's thoughts on Egypt or his lost potential during those lonely days taking care of sheep. The man who would have been prince of Egypt now finds himself alone in the wilderness.

Leadership Lesson: Solitude can be a valuable experience in preparation for leadership.

In the wilderness of Midian, God prepares Moses to be the deliverer of Israel. Wiersbe says, "Moses's forty years of waiting and working prepared him for a lifetime of faithful ministry."[4] Could God be using a season of solitude to prepare you for the mission of a lifetime?

David Brooks writes that failure teaches us who we are and brings about moral renewal if that failure leads us to "a period of solitude, in the wilderness, where self-reflection can occur." In the wilderness, our way of proving our worth is stripped away. Brooks says, "Belden Lane asks in *Backpacking with the Saints*, What happens where there is no audience, nothing he can achieve? He crumbles. The ego dissolves. 'Only then is he able to be loved.'"[5]

There are some truths that are best discovered in solitude. The wilderness can teach us the vital skill of how to serve without recognition. It also helps us develop confidence that is not based on achievements.[6]

Questions for Leadership Development

1. What places and experiences has God used to prepare you for leadership?

2. In what ways has solitude played a role in your past or present preparation for leadership?

3. In what ways can your leadership responsibility be compared to shepherding?

— SEVEN —

THE BURNING BUSH, PART 1: THE CALL TO LEADERSHIP

Earth's crammed with heaven,
And every common bush afire with God,
But only he who sees takes off his shoes;
The rest sit round and pluck blackberries.
Elizabeth Barrett Browning

In her work highlighting the leadership of four U.S. presidents (Lincoln, both Roosevelts, and L. Johnson), historian Doris Goodwin asks, "Do leaders shape the times or do the times summon their leaders?" She continues, "If there is not oppression, you do not get the great Emancipator." Goodwin further observes the importance of resilience in leadership growth: "Scholars who have studied the development of leaders have situated resilience, the ability to sustain ambition in the face of frustration, at the heart of potential leadership growth. More important than what happened to them was how they responded to these reversals, how they managed in various ways to put themselves back together, how these watershed experiences at first impeded, then deepened, and finally and decisively molded their leadership."[1]

Moses's forty years as shepherd not only hone his resilience, but they also enable him to gain familiarity with the wilderness terrain, reach a level of self-awareness that solitude enables, and become accustomed to caring for needs other than his own. God is shaping a leader for the challenge of the times.

Yet, as Moses tends his father-in-law's sheep, he undoubtedly considers the myriad ways these forty years of his life have differed from the first forty years of his life. Moses is completely out of the loop and away from the action. He has traded the intrigue of the Egyptian palace for the solitude of the wilderness. He has gone from the center of the world's culture to the middle of one of the world's forgotten places.

Making sure sheep are fed and watered, caring for their needs, and taking care of their injuries and scratches can become rather routine, especially if you have been doing it for four decades. Perhaps every now and then a wolf comes around and things get interesting for a while, but most of the time it is a dull responsibility. Sheep are stubborn, high-maintenance creatures. They get lost. They need protection. They must have food and water. Tending sheep can be a dreary responsibility; Moses is mired in the mundane.

With the sunrise filling his eyes and the bleating of sheep filling his ears, Moses has no idea what is about to happen to him. He is simply minding his own business (or, perhaps more accurately, Jethro's business) when God suddenly and unexpectedly calls him away from what he is doing and sets the path of his life on a new trajectory.

God initiates the contact. Moses is not seeking God. God is seeking Moses, and God finds Moses on the far side of the desert. Now God must get Moses's attention, and he chooses to do so through a bush that is burning without being consumed.

Leadership Lesson: It is harder for God to get our attention than it is for us to get God's attention.

One problem with seasons that are mundane is that expectations lower and anticipation wanes. We are not looking for anything significant to happen. How many burning bushes do we walk by before we notice one?

There are some places that are easier for God to get our attention. Mission trips, church camps, and youth retreats draw us away from our routines and make it easier to be aware of God's presence. It can be difficult to be sensitive to divine engagements in the midst of the ordinary and the routine, but noticing burning bushes can make all the difference in our lives.

The common bush begins to shine with fire. Fire becomes a frequent sign of God's presence during Exodus (see 13:21; 19:18; 24:17). The bush burns, but it is not consumed. The blaze flares up, but the shrub is not destroyed. The source of fuel is not exhausted. It is enough to intrigue Moses, capture his attention, prompt him to investigate, and draw him in closer.

Leadership Lesson: God is able to light fires that do not burn out.

You may need to be reminded that God can light fires that stay lit. This is a burning bush that does not burn out or burn up. Your call, your experience, and your passion do not have to burn out. Marriage fires can stay lit. Ministry fires can continue to burn brightly. Vocational passion can remain ardent. The burning bush reminds leaders that God's resources are limitless.

The voice of God breaks the stillness of the wilderness with words that draw Moses in even farther: "Moses! Moses!" God calls Moses by name twice, suggesting urgency. And Moses responds, "Here I am" (Exodus 3:4).

God gives Moses two commands: 1) Don't come any closer, and 2) take off your sandals (v. 5). Both relate to Moses finding himself on holy ground. What begins as a curiosity in Exodus 3:3 turns into a cause for reverence. As one writer puts it, "Moses is getting a crash course in holy etiquette."[2] The holy presence of God demands a respectful distance. "Don't come any closer" is a restriction on the approach to divinity that will occur time and time again during the exodus.

Moses must remove his shoes before he comes any closer to God. This ancient Near Eastern sign of removing one's sandals is a sign of reverence, humility, and submission. Joshua is commanded to do the same in Joshua 5:15. One does not enter into God's presence casually, without reverence.

Moses removes his shoes in acknowledgment that he is standing on holy ground. But perhaps God also has Moses remove his shoes so that Moses will be as close as possible to holiness. Just as the ground has been separated for God's use and called holy, so Moses is also being separated for God's use. Perhaps God is saying, *Moses, I don't want anything separating you from the holy. Take off your shoes.*

Leadership Lesson: God calls leaders to both respect and experience the holy.

Four times in the book of Leviticus we find the words, "Be holy, because I am holy" (11:44, 45; 19:2; 20:26). God's holiness is his defining quality. The idea of holiness usually has to do with righteousness, goodness, and purity. It also involves the glory and majesty of

God. Another aspect of holiness is the idea of separation. Holy ground is special ground. It is set apart, different from surrounding ground. When "holy" is used to describe humans, it also means set apart—separated *from* sin, *for* God's special purpose.

A key component of Moses's call is God's concern for his people. Exodus 3:7–10 reveals several ways in which God identifies and connects with human need. First, God sees and hears human need: "I have indeed *seen* the misery of my people in Egypt. I have *heard* them crying out because of their slave drivers" (v. 7a, emphases added).

What misery does God see and hear? God sees a people displaced by famine and oppressed by a pharaoh. God hears their groans as they sweat over ovens making bricks. God sees the whips oppressors use on their backs and the lifeless bodies of babies floating in the Nile. God has eyes that see and ears that hear the needs of people.

Leadership Lesson: **God calls leaders to see what he sees and hear what he hears.**

Today, God sees the misery of girls and women enslaved by the sex trade. God sees the misery of single parents trapped in poverty. God sees the misery of those oppressed by drugs, alcohol, and pornography. God sees the misery of the homeless, the helpless, and the hopeless.

God hears the cries of those enslaved by sin. God hears the cries of children who have lost the security of a two-parent home. God hears the cries of Christian leaders who long to see the Spirit move in their congregations. In all these things, God enables leaders to see what he sees and hear what he hears.

———

Second, because God sees and hears, God is concerned and *acts*: "I am concerned about their suffering. So I have come down to rescue them from the hand of the Egyptians" (vv. 7b–8a). God cares about suffering people so much that he does something about it. He not only cares about people, but he also acts on their behalf. Well aware of the situation, he prepares to intervene, saying, *I see. I hear. I care. And I have come down to rescue them and bring them up.* This is the God who comes down in order to bring people up!

———

Leadership Lesson: The call to leadership is an invitation to "come down" so that others can be lifted up.

The temptation of leaders is to get this backwards. We'd much rather be lifted high than brought low. We'd much rather be served than serve. However, leaders are invited to bow low so others might be raised up.

God enables the leaders he calls to act like God acts. This isn't the last time God will come down to rescue people. God's most awesome rescue operation is seen in the incarnation of Jesus Christ. Jesus comes down to earth to rescue us from sin and bring us up to salvation. In Philippians 2:5–7, Paul proclaims this truth in a riveting way. "In your relationships with one another, have the same mindset as Christ Jesus: Who, being in very nature God, did not consider equality with God something to be used to his own advantage; rather, he made himself nothing by taking the very nature of a servant."

God has modeled for us what it means to come down in order to lift people up and lead them to deliverance.

———

THE CALL TO LEADERSHIP

God is not only aware of the human condition; he is also willing to do something about it. God cares about the suffering Hebrews so much that he takes action, calling his servant Moses.

Leadership Lesson: **The call to leadership is not about the abilities of a leader but about the needs of the people. The "why" of your call is more important than the "how."**

Moses's call originates in God's concern for his people. The "how" of Moses's call is contained in Exodus 3:1–6. The story of Moses and the burning bush is the quintessential call-to-leadership story. Some leaders have a burning-bush kind of story—memorable and astonishing. Other leaders have more of a smoldering-shrub kind of story—not a single moment seared into our consciousness but instead a growing awareness that God is opening a door.

The "why" of Moses's call is contained in Exodus 3:7–10. In this passage, we learn about the God who calls us and why. Your call to leadership is God's response to someone's need!

There are two kinds of leaders: those who never get over the "how" of their call—the burning bush; and those who never get over the "why" of their call—the burning need.

Why does God call women and men to leadership? Because he has seen enough. Because he has heard enough. And because he cares enough to do something about human need. What he has decided to do is call leaders to partner with him in delivering humanity from oppression and distress.

What matters most is not *how* Moses is called. What matters most is *why* Moses is called. Moses is God's answer to the cries of the Hebrews. Likewise, what matters most is not how you were called. What matters most is why you were called. You are God's answer to something. God calls us not because we have great gifts and abilities but because the world has great need.

God works through human agents to address bondage, exploitation, injustice, and other inhumane activities. As Junia Pokrifka says, "The mission of the church . . . is to champion the cause of the powerless, speak for the voiceless, and confront the oppressors, insisting on God's demand for the freedom of the oppressed."[3]

God has a mission for Moses. God says, *Moses, I am sending you. Pack your bags. You are starting on a journey that will rock your world.* Moses is about to embark on the adventure of his life—full of drama and challenges, frustrations and miracles.

Questions for Leadership Development

1. What resonates most with you in your call to leadership—the "how" or the "why" of the call?

2. How can leaders guard against burnout?

3. What human need might God be calling you to address?

— EIGHT —

THE BURNING BUSH, PART 2: THE VOICE OF LEADERSHIP

*It is laid upon the stammering to bring
the voice of heaven to earth.*

Gerhard Von Rad[1]

At the burning bush, Moses's dual mission is revealed: carry God's word to Pharaoh, and carry God's people to the promised land.

Leadership Lesson: The mission of every God-called leader is to take God's people from where they are to where God is calling them to be.

God gives Moses a simple mission: *Lead my people from where they are—Egypt—to where I have called them to be—the promised land.* Simple. But not easy. For us it means taking God's people from where they are—spiritually, emotionally, attitudinally, and in some cases where they are physically and culturally—to where God is calling them to be. Simple. But not easy. Where is God calling you to take people?

In response to God's call, Moses begins to argue, giving excuses for why he should not to go back to Egypt. Moses understands the tremendous risk associated with obeying God's call, and he responds by asking questions, making excuses, and raising objections. He asks four questions, the first two of which are questions of identity, followed by a question related to credibility and ending with a question related to ability. Then Moses offers a final objection.

The Question of a Leader's Identity: Who Am I?

First, Moses doubts himself, asking, "Who am I?" (Exodus 3:11). Moses wonders how his identity qualifies him for the task to which God has called him. Moses's rhetorical question "conveys his unworthiness, unpreparedness, inadequacy, and perhaps his fear."[2]

Leadership Lesson: Self-awareness is important in leadership.

Doris Goodwin says, "The self-awareness to soberly analyze your own strengths and compensate for your weaknesses is a critical leadership attribute."[3] Leaders tend to be overconfident or underconfident, and Moses is the latter. An accurate assessment of your own gifts and abilities as well as your personality and strengths is important to leadership effectiveness.

Moses's words, "Who am I, that I should go to Pharaoh?" (v. 11) reflect more than humility. His words are both a question of self-awareness and a statement of inadequacy. The question reflects a level of self-deprecation inconsistent with one who has been appointed by God. Moses is expressing feelings of insufficiency, hesitation, and reluctance.

In response, God assures Moses of his presence. God's response to Moses's first question does not, at first, appear to be fitting. But upon deeper reflection, it becomes obvious that God is clarifying that human adequacy is not the question. Humans *are* inadequate, but God is both adequate and present.

Moses contends, "Why send me? I can't do this." God seems to be answering, *It doesn't matter who you are. Of course you're inadequate. I'm the one who is adequate, and I am with you.* Moses's insufficiency is countered by divine presence (v. 12).

Leadership Lesson: **The best response to feelings of human insufficiency is the assurance of divine presence.**

God promises us his presence. It is noteworthy that God counters Moses's question of identity by assuring Moses of his presence. This will become a recurring theme throughout the exodus story. Moses will do almost anything as long as he knows God is with him. At the very beginning, God give him the assurance, "Certainly I will be with you" (Exodus 3:12, NASB). God promises his presence. Present "not merely some time and somewhere but in every now and in every here."[4]

This promise echoes through both the Old and New Testaments. The words "never will I leave you; never will I forsake you" (Deuteronomy 31:6; Hebrews 13:5) continue to inspire leaders who are aware of their own inadequacies for leadership.

God answers Moses's first question by saying, *It doesn't matter who you are. The only thing that matters is who I am, and who I have promised to be to you.*

Then Moses asks, "Well, who are you?"

The Question of God's Identity: What Is Your Name?

Moses's second question to God is "What is your name?" Moses is seeking clarification on God's identity. He doesn't even know God's name. How can he be expected to lead God's people if he doesn't know God's name?

Moses assumes the Israelites will ask him who this God is who is calling them out of Egypt. Moses's credibility with the Hebrews will be severely impacted if he cannot even tell them the name of the God who is revealing himself to him.

Moses asks to be allowed to know God's name. His desire is, at heart, a desire to know something of the nature and of the being of God. The only way people can really worship God is if God reveals himself to them and tells them his name. After all, it is difficult to worship an unknown God.

God proclaims his name as Jehovah: "I AM WHO I AM" (Exodus 3:14). The name God gives Moses is called the *tetragrammaton,* or "four letters," because in the Hebrew text it is the four-letter name for God. Originally, written Hebrew did not have vowels, only consonants, so it would have appeared as *YHWH* in the original Hebrew text. The Jews consider the name to be so holy that it is blasphemous to speak it. Instead, they substitute *Adonai,* which simply means "Lord." *YHWH* has been translated as either *Jehovah* or *Yahweh.*

God reveals his name as *YHWH,* which means: "I will be that which I will be," "I will be present," or "I will take place."[5] The four consonants come from the verb *to be.* He is a God of activity or action. There on Horeb, in front of a bush that burns but is not consumed, God tells Moses God's own name. Armed with that knowledge, Moses is to go forth.

Leadership Lesson: Two questions of utmost importance to a leader are the question of self-awareness and the question of God-awareness.

Of the two, the question of God-awareness is most important. Knowing the name of God is important, but knowing God himself is of greater importance. It is the impulse of humans, even genuinely religious people, to want to get God under their own control.[6] The leader's knowledge of God must not be used for manipulative effect. Leaders must avoid the temptation to use their knowledge of God to promote or advance their own purposes.

The Question of a Leader's Credibility: What If They Won't Follow Me?

Moses's third question reveals his fear that the Hebrews will not believe him. First, Moses doubts himself. Now, Moses doubts the people God is calling him to lead: "What if they do not believe me or listen to me and say, 'The LORD did not appear to you'?" (Exodus 4:1). Moses is concerned not only about his lack of qualifications but also about his lack of credibility: "I don't think I can do this, and neither will anyone else." He is concerned about his credentials and being rejected by the Israelites. It's worth noting that Moses is not concerned with whether *Pharaoh* will recognize his authority but with whether *Israel* will.

Leadership Lesson: It is legitimate for you as a leader to desire acceptance by the group you are called to.

Moses's concern about whether the Israelites will accept his leadership is valid. Most every vocation has a peer-review process to evaluate effectiveness and legitimacy. Peter Enns says, "God's call on our lives must be checked or confirmed by the whole. For example, if someone feels called to be a pastor, we do not just take that person's word for it. Every denomination that I know of has some sort of process, whether formal (seminary, ordination exams) or less formal (a perception of the candidate's spiritual maturity and ability to lead people), whereby that all is scrutinized. Bypassing that process can have disastrous effects."[7]

God gives Moses three signs—three miracles to perform in Egypt—to convince the Jewish elders that he is truly God's chosen servant. The first sign, as told in Exodus 4:2-5, involves something that Moses is found holding in his hand when God first speaks to him.

"What is that in your hand?" God asks.

"A staff," replies Moses.

"Throw it on the ground," God commands.

Moses obeys, and the wooden staff instantly becomes a snake. Why a snake? Perhaps because the snake represents a sign of Egyptian royal authority.

Moses immediately turns and runs.

"Stretch out your hand and pick up the snake by the tail," God commands.

Moses complies, and the snake turns back into a staff. While Pharaoh consistently gives into fear throughout the story, Moses will be given the opportunity to overcome his fear, beginning with this act of picking up a writhing snake.

Leadership Question: What is already in your hand?

At the point of being called to leadership, leaders already possess gifts and assets that God can repurpose. Asking the question, "What's in your hand?" is powerful. God may have already equipped you with everything needed to fulfill his calling in your life. What might God be able to accomplish through his power with the resources already at hand? What do you already have that God wants to use or transform? A shepherd's staff seems pitiful next to the sword, gavel, or scepter Moses once may have held. But what Moses now has in his hand will be enough. God will repurpose Moses's staff, accomplishing astounding things with it. God can use mundane, ordinary, common, and insignificant things to achieve his grand purposes. Whatever gifts we have, when turned over to God, can be used by him in a powerful way. In the same way, Moses's staff, just a tool made of wood, becomes a mighty instrument of God's power.

The second sign God gives Moses to prove himself to the Israelite elders is found in Exodus 4:6-8. God tells Moses to put his hand inside his cloak. When he pulls it out, it turns white with leprosy. When Moses puts his hand back in his cloak, his hand becomes healthy and whole again. Peter Enns says that the significance of this sign "seems to be authority over disease and sickness, and as such may anticipate the infliction of pain in some of the plagues."[8]

The third sign, found in Exodus 4:9, is the turning of water to blood. Like the first sign, turning water to blood will be repeated before the Egyptians. It is a preview of the first plague (see Exodus 7:14–24). Because Egypt's life force is the Nile, this sign signifies God's power over the elements. This sign will also condemn the Egyptians for their crime of infanticide in the Nile.

The Question of a Leader's Ability: What If My Gifts Aren't Sufficient?

Moses's final objection introduces the question of ability. Perhaps Moses continues to resist God's call, as some scholars suggest, because "he assumes that he is playing the central role in the deliverance of the Israelites . . . What Moses does not yet understand is that God cares more about Israel's deliverance than he does, and God is fully capable of directing the means to bring this about. It is God who will bring his people out of Egypt. He will display his might precisely by working through weak and ordinary means. Moses has not yet learned that salvation is of the Lord."[9]

Here is Moses's final plea: "Pardon your servant, Lord. I have never been eloquent, neither in the past nor since you have spoken to your servant. I am slow of speech and tongue" (Exodus 4:10). Moses's last excuse is his lack of ability in public speaking.

There seem to be two main theories on Moses's lack of eloquence. The first is that during his many years in Midian he lost his mastery of the Egyptian language. Maybe he no longer feels equipped to impress Pharaoh with his sophisticated discourse.[10] The second theory is that he has difficulty pronouncing certain words due to some kind of speech impediment. Either way, he does not feel he is as eloquent as he needs to be if he is to act as God's spokesman.

Leadership Lesson: It is easy for leaders to focus on what they lack rather than what they possess.

Spiritual leaders have the privilege of helping women and men discover that our credibility is linked not primarily to what *we* can do but to what God chooses to do in and through us. When our focus is on ourselves rather than God, it is easy to become timid and feel incapable. Our boldness should not be based on our own capabilities, talents, or abilities. Our confidence should be based not in ourselves, or even primarily in our message, but in the one who has called us and given us the message. Both timidity and pride are due to a focus on ourselves.

Each of Moses's excuses focuses on a lack—a lack of confidence, a lack of knowledge, a lack of credibility, or a lack of eloquence. What Moses does have are God's presence and God's promise.

In an age when we tend to focus on leadership strengths, perhaps an acknowledgment that God most often chooses to work through weakness provides a needed balance. Moses appears to be chosen not in spite of his limitation but because of it. Moses's limitation is seen as an opportunity for God to display God's lack of limitation. God often chooses to work through weakness rather than strength. This is Paul's contention in 2 Corinthians 12:10: "For when I am weak, then I am strong." God uses human weaknesses for his glory.

God is greater than our inadequacies, lack of experience, and lack of talent. Salvation is in God's hands, and he will work through whomever he chooses. Salvation comes from the Lord, not from a leader.

The Affirmation of a Leader's Voice

In Exodus 4, we read that God must remind Moses that he has created him. "Who gave human beings their mouths? Who makes them deaf or mute? Who gives them sight or makes them blind? Is it not I, the LORD?" (v. 11). Of course, God can easily overcome any lack, including Moses's lack of eloquence. But instead of curing Moses of his speech problem, God affirms Moses's mouth. He has chosen to use Moses's voice, lacking though it may be. Far from being an unfortunate limitation, "Moses's mouth is exactly what God has chosen."[11] God is identifying Moses's mouth as the instrument he has chosen to make his will and his word known.

Jewish scholar Avivah Gottlieb Zornberg says that "when God reassures Moses ('They will listen to your voice') God is not just making a promise; he is making a condition: 'Only if you speak with your voice will they listen and join you in challenging Pharaoh.' The whole scenario of redemption depends on this one condition: Moses's voice must be heard. The elders hear God's words, but in the wrong voice, and they are not inspired to accompany Moses to the palace. Instead, Moses and Aaron go alone . . ."[12]

Moses continues to resist his weakness. He is happy to let Aaron speak. But God has chosen to use Moses's voice. Moses wants God to use Aaron's voice. But Aaron's voice isn't going to work with the elders of Israel, and Aaron's voice isn't going to work with Pharaoh. The words Aaron utters will be in Aaron's voice. Zornberg says, "The whole scenario of redemption depends on this one condition: Moses's voice must be heard. In the event, Moses refuses to speak and Aaron is delegated to convey God's words. So the elders hear God's words, but in the wrong voice. The result is that the scenario of redemption falters. The elders are not inspired to accompany Moses to the palace. Instead, Moses and Aaron go alone."[13]

God wants Moses's voice. Moses's voice will convey the tone and rhythm of redemption that God desires others to hear. Moses's voice is necessary in all its inadequacy. The people of Israel need to hear Moses's voice. Pharaoh needs to hear Moses's voice.

Leadership Lesson: **As a leader, you must use your own voice, not another's. Don't copy sermons or mimic other leaders or preachers. Speak your own, God-given words in your own, God-given voice.**

A leader's voice is as important as a leader's words. Moses's voice is necessary in all its inadequacy. The people of Israel need to hear his voice. For those of us who serve the church as overseers, this has significant implications for our work placing leaders. We need to be asking, "Who needs to hear this leader's voice?" We also have the privilege of using our own voices to help those called by God find their voices. It's powerful when words are united with voice.

Final Objection: "There's Someone Better for the Job"

As mentioned earlier, Moses's final objection is that he is not as qualified as others, so someone else should be chosen for this mission. Moses is polite. He doesn't come right out and say, "I don't want to do it." Rather, he suggests, "Please send someone else" (Exodus 4:13). Moses knows it needs to be done. But Moses does not want to go.

Leadership Lesson: **There will almost always be someone else more qualified than you.**

Can someone else do it better? Probably. That's no reason to resist what God has called you to do. Moses suggests, "Aaron has a better voice! Use him!" But the question should not be, "Does someone have a better voice?" The question should be, "Who needs to hear *your* voice?"

⸻

God does not become angry with Moses until this fifth challenge. God is patient up to that point. And even in his anger, God is gracious. Aaron becomes God's compromise. God gives in to Moses's stubbornness. Just as Moses is to be God's spokesman, Aaron will be Moses's spokesman. Moses and Aaron will become a team, but it is not an equal partnership. "Moses is still God's chosen instrument. Aaron is only a concession."[14] In time, Moses will find his voice. And by the time Deuteronomy rolls around, what a voice it has become.

The conversation between Moses and God ends somewhat abruptly in Exodus 4:17: "But take this staff in your hand so you can perform the signs with it." Or, in other words, "Don't forget your staff, Moses." It seems like a strange ending to an intense and dramatic encounter. Perhaps God wants to remind Moses that, while he is about to leave behind forever the world of shepherding, the same traits that made him effective as a leader of sheep will serve him well as a leader of people. Moses's staff will play a prominent role in the plague narratives. God will use the simple tool of a lowly occupation to bring about the redemption and deliverance of his people.

God has already given Moses what he needs to accomplish the mission God has for him: his voice, a staff, and the assurance that God will be with him.

"Don't forget your staff, Moses."

Questions for Leadership Development

1. Where is God calling you to take the people you serve?

2. How does a leader develop self-awareness?

3. How does a leader cultivate an awareness of God's presence?

4. What's in your hand? How has God already equipped you?

— NINE —

PHARAOH, PART 2: HARD-HEARTED LEADERSHIP

*Blessed is the one who always trembles
before God, but whoever hardens
their heart falls into trouble.*

Proverbs 28:14

*Today, if you hear his voice,
do not harden your hearts.*

Hebrews 4:7b

When Moses reaches Egypt, he meets with the elders of the Hebrew community. The people believe Moses and his report and when they hear that God is concerned about them, they respond with worship (Exodus 4:31).

Moses is instructed to go to Pharaoh and request permission to take a three-day journey into the wilderness to offer sacrifices to the Lord. He is also told to "perform before Pharaoh all the wonders I [the Lord] have given you the power to do" (Exodus 4:21). The Lord tells Moses that Pharaoh will need to be compelled, and that God will provide the mighty hand that will convince Pharaoh to relent.

It is amazing that Moses even gains an audience with Pharaoh. Perhaps he remembers enough of palace protocol to know how to arrange such a meeting. Moses is granted an appointment with the Egyptian leader and makes the bold request that the Hebrew slaves be allowed to hold a festival in the wilderness.

The first request Moses makes is not received well. Pharaoh asks two questions: Why should I obey the Lord? (see Exodus 5:2) and Why should the work stop? (see v. 4). The labor the Israelites are supplying is a great economic benefit to Egypt, and Pharaoh isn't about to give that up. So, instead of giving the Israelites a break from their labor, Pharaoh makes it even harder. He aims to intensify the hardship of the Israelites by making their work unbearable. He demands that they maintain their daily quota of brick production, but he will no longer provide straw to make the bricks. They will have to find the straw on their own while maintaining the daily output.

Moses's first appearance before Pharaoh ends in disaster. Not only does Pharaoh refuse to let the people go, but he also responds by making their lives even more difficult, and blaming Moses and Aaron for it. Pharaoh considers their request for a furlough to be evidence of their laziness. Rather than agreeing to Moses's request that the Hebrews hold a festival to the Lord in the wilderness, Pharaoh instead decides to double down on the oppression of the Hebrews.

Although Moses and Aaron are initially well received by the Israelites, their welcome sours after a devastating first meeting with Pharaoh. Instead of granting freedom, Pharaoh only intensifies his cruelty. As a result, the Israelites become resentful of Moses and Aaron.

Leadership Lesson: Sometimes things get worse before they get better.

The only achievement of Moses and Aaron in their first encounter with Pharaoh is to make the lives of their fellow Israelites even harder. Far from rescuing his people, Moses has only caused a bad situation to become worse.

While Moses's mission will ultimately be realized, it will not be immediate. We see a similar development in the story of Joseph (see Genesis 37–50). Joseph is sold into slavery by his brothers, which is bad enough. But then he is falsely accused and imprisoned. A bad situation became even worse.

There are often setbacks, challenges, and discouragements in achieving the mission God has given us. Discerning when to persevere and when to change tactics is key to leadership. Meyer says, "We must never suppose that the difficulties that confront us indicate we are not on God's path and doing his work. Indeed, the contrary is generally the case."[1]

Leaders often discover that challenging times get worse before they get better. One often experiences Good Friday before Easter Sunday. Wisdom and discernment are needed to know when to persist and when to change direction. Don't give up too soon. Give God time to work. Stay the course.

The Hebrew slaves are unable to keep up with the demand and fulfill their daily quota. When their work becomes unbearable, the Hebrew foremen bypass Moses and Aaron as intermediaries and take their complaint directly to Pharaoh: "Why have you treated your servants this way? Your servants are given no straw, yet we are told, 'Make bricks!' Your servants are being beaten, but the fault is with your own people" (Exodus 5:15-16).

When they appeal to Pharaoh for mercy, they are called "lazy" and told to get back to work (v. 17). Pharaoh wants to make certain they know exactly who to blame for their latest woes. He seeks to turn the Israelites against Moses and Aaron, whom Pharaoh regards as two rabble rousers inciting rebellion. Pharaoh tells the Israelite foremen that it is not the Egyptian taskmasters who are to blame for this burden but Moses and Aaron, who keep saying, "Let us go and sacrifice to the Lord" (v. 17). As a result, Moses and Aaron lose even more credibility with the Israelites.

Pharaoh's crafty response is designed to disparage Moses's credibility with his own people, and it succeeds. The Israelite overseers then blame Moses and Aaron for the mess they are in: "May the LORD look on you and judge you! You have made us obnoxious to Pharaoh and his officials and have put a sword in their hand to kill us" (v. 21).

Moses has been miserably ineffective. He has not made things better; in fact, he has made them worse. His responding prayer is filled with frustration. For the first time in the Bible, God is asked, "Why?" Moses asks him twice.[2]

Leadership Lesson: It is easier to blame someone else than to take personal responsibility.

It's been that way since the first sin. Eve blamed the serpent. Adam blamed Eve and then God. We'll see Aaron play the blame game in chapter 20. There is always enough blame to go around. The Israelite foremen blame Pharaoh. Pharaoh blames Moses and Aaron. The Hebrews blame Moses and Aaron. Moses blames God. Everyone seems to be looking for someone else to blame. Affixing blame may ease one's sense of responsibility, but it never makes the situation better. Good leaders don't place blame. Good leaders take responsibility.

The discouragement and harsh labor the Israelites are experiencing makes it difficult for them to listen to Moses. The foremen no longer blame Pharaoh for the decree; now they blame Moses. The theme of grumbling emerges in Exodus 5:21. It is a theme that will be replayed often, in various settings and for various reasons, over the next forty years. Opposition to God and his chosen deliverer is a common refrain throughout the Israelite exodus.

Moses and Aaron have gone once to Pharaoh and failed. Not only has Pharaoh refused to let the people go, but he has also imposed greater burdens on them. Now God instructs Moses and Aaron to demand a second time that the Israelites be allowed to go. This time, Moses employs the sign God has directed him to demonstrate (see Exodus 7:8–13). Aaron throws his staff on the ground, and it becomes a squirming snake. It's important to note that serpents were one of the special creatures in Egyptian religion. The cobra was symbolic of immortality,[3] which is why the headdress of the pharaoh would have resembled this creature.[4] But after Aaron turns his staff into a snake, the sign is duplicated by Pharaoh's court magicians, so Pharaoh is not swayed. Pharaoh is stubborn, and his stubbornness will be characterized over and over again as "hardness of heart"—the condition in which a person deliberately rejects the gracious offer of God to be part of his or her life.

Pharaoh will not let the Israelites go because Pharaoh's heart is unyielding and hard, and it will only get harder. But is it hard because Pharaoh makes it hard or because God makes it hard? The answer is yes. There are times when the Bible says Pharaoh hardens his own heart. There are other times when the Bible says that God hardens Pharaoh's heart (see Exodus 7:13, 22; 8:15, 19, 32; 9:7, 12, 34; 10:20, 27; 11:10). This is the tension of the story.

God hardens Pharaoh's heart in order to demonstrate his power. Pharaoh chooses to disregard God's will and therefore hardens his own heart. As one writer puts it, "God can harden hearts simply by allowing us to go our own way. He does not have to intervene in a special way; our hearts are hard and get harder by themselves. If God does not work in our lives with softening grace, hardening is the inevitable result. This is what the theological term reprobation means. Reprobation is when God allows people to go their own way."[5] In Romans 9, Paul quotes Exodus 9:16 and concludes, "Therefore God has mercy on whom he wants to have mercy, and he hardens whom he wants to harden" (v. 18).

What does it mean that Pharaoh's heart was *hardened*? Junia Pokrifka says, "The expression 'hardening one's heart' can be understood in terms of Yahweh giving Pharaoh over to the maximum extent of Pharaoh's own pride, arrogance, defiance, and irrationality, until Pharaoh and Egypt reap the full consequences of the century-long diabolical treatment of the Israelites."[6] Perhaps God is simply enabling Pharaoh to continue to be the arrogant, unrelenting leader he is, and the natural result is a heart that becomes harder and harder.

Leadership Lesson: Leaders must guard against hard-heartedness.

The tension between God's sovereignty and humanity's free will is one we struggle with. At times Pharaoh hardens his own heart. At other times God does it for him. To "harden your heart" means that, even when you see clear evidence of God's hand at work, you still resist God by refusing to accept his Word and do his will, demanding one's own will be done instead. Hardness of heart can also mean "to resist [God] by showing ingratitude and disobedience and not having any fear of the Lord or of his judgements."[7] Grace resisted always results in a hardened heart. Grace received always results in a changed heart. God has the power to transform even a hardened heart. The prophet Ezekiel reminds us of God's power to provide a new heart: "I will give you a new heart and put a new spirit in you; I will remove from you your heart of stone and give you a heart of flesh" (36:26).

Pokrifka says the hardening of Pharaoh's heart appears to have taken place in three stages.

In the beginning of the plague narrative, the text simply describes Pharaoh's heart as being hardened, resolute, and unyielding, without saying who hardened it. . . . In the middle (mostly in the second through the seventh plagues), Pharaoh is said to willingly harden his own heart (8:15, 32 [11, 28 HB] 9:34-35), making it increasingly calloused against severer plagues. In the last phase (sixth, eighth through tenth, the Red Sea), God is described as hardening Pharaoh's heart . . . to ensure his continued resistance until the complete fulfillment of God's divine purposes.[8]

This is the mystery of the paradoxical relationship between God's sovereignty and human responsibility. Pharaoh is responsible for his own sinful actions. He stubbornly refuses to let the Israelites go. It will take catastrophe after catastrophe to break the pharaoh's iron-plated heart. Those catastrophes are on the horizon. When the sign of the snake is ignored, the plagues commence.

Questions for Leadership Development

1. In challenging times, how can leaders discern when to persist and when to change direction?

2. What might be the indicators that a leader's heart is becoming hard?

3. How can a leader guard against hard-heartedness?

— TEN —

THE PLAGUES AND THE PASSOVER: GOD'S PROVISION

Christ our Redeemer died on the cross,
Died for the sinner, paid all his due . . .
When I see the blood,
When I see the blood,
I will pass, I will pass over you.
John G. Foote[1]

While only a few lines are given to telling the early life story of Moses, nearly five chapters (Exodus 7:14–11:10) are devoted to the ten plagues. The word "plague" means "a blow" or "a stroke," and indicates that the hand of the Lord is punishing the Egyptians.

The purpose of the plagues is fourfold. First, the plagues are God's judgment against the gods of Egypt and evidence of his power over them. Pharaoh is a man who believes the Egyptian gods are the most powerful on earth. The plagues will cause him to reevaluate that belief. Each of the plagues can be seen as an attack on a different Egyptian deity. In ancient Egypt, there are many gods and goddesses—about eighty—clustered around three main sources of Egyptian life: the Nile, the land, and the sun.[2] The plagues are directed against these three sources and the gods and goddesses of Egypt that are grouped around them. The first two plagues are directed against the gods and goddesses of the Nile and everything associated with the Nile. The next four are directed against the gods and goddesses of the land. The final four are directed against the sky and everything associated with it.

The second purpose of the plagues is to soften Pharaoh's hard heart. Like a sledgehammer increasing in force, the plagues increase in intensity to break Pharaoh's resistance. The plagues are designed to convince him to release God's people. For that to happen, Pharaoh's heart must be softened.

The third purpose of the plagues is to judge and punish the Egyptians for oppressing and murdering the Israelites. All of Egypt has benefited from slavery, and all of Egypt is made to suffer for the stubbornness of Pharaoh.

The fourth—and ultimate—purpose of the plagues is to deliver Israel. The plagues will end as soon as the exodus begins.

The Final Plague: The Death of the Firstborn
Exodus 11:1–10; 12:29–32

With one mighty act, God could destroy both Pharaoh and Egypt (see Exodus 9:15), but God chooses to give them many opportunities to repent. They experience water turned to blood, frogs, gnats, flies, the death of their livestock, boils, hail, locusts, and darkness. Nevertheless, the previous plagues have not produced repentance in Pharaoh. Instead, he has increasingly hardened his heart in hostile resistance.

Once again, the Lord speaks to Moses, but this time he announces there will be one last plague that will finally convince Pharaoh to not only let the Israelites go but also to drive them out completely. In preparation, the Israelites are to ask their neighbors for articles of gold and silver. Amazingly, a consequence of the plagues is that the Egyptians have become favorably disposed toward the Israelites and Moses is "highly regarded" by both Pharaoh's officials and the Egyptian population (11:3).

Before the final plague, Moses makes five announcements:

1. Something is going to happen at midnight (v. 4).
2. All of Egypt's firstborn sons will die (v. 5).
3. This will be a national tragedy (v. 6).
4. Israel will be protected (v. 7).
5. There will be an exodus (v. 8).[3]

At the very beginning of their conflict, Moses warns Pharaoh that the way he treats God's firstborn will determine how God treats Egypt's firstborn (Exodus 4:22–23). Pharaoh decreed the death of the Jewish male babies, so God decrees the death of the Egyptian firstborn. "Since Israel is God's firstborn son, the appropriate punishment against Egypt for harming Israel is for God to harm Egypt's firstborn son."[4]

Moses delivers the news of a final plague to Pharaoh with added passion, for he is "hot with anger" (Exodus 11:8). Pharaoh is told that at about midnight the Lord will go throughout Egypt and every firstborn son will die. These deaths will impact the Egyptians from the greatest to the least—even the firstborn of the cattle will die.

As the angel of death comes through the land to slay all the firstborn sons of the Egyptians, the Hebrews gather in their houses, protected by the blood of lambs that have been killed. At midnight the Lord strikes down all the firstborn of Egypt. The whole of Egypt awakens to the horror and shock of the deaths of their loved ones. Pharaoh and all the Egyptians are roused during the night by the wailing, for there is someone dead in every house in Egypt. The grief of Egypt is audible and dreadful. But there is a distinction between the Egyptians and the Israelites. Whereas Egypt is marked by wails and cries of loss, not even a dog barks among the Israelites. The terrible cries and anguish that have marked the Israelites' oppression now mark the sorrow and loss of the Egyptians.

Leadership Lesson: God is sovereign.

God alone—the creator and judge of the universe—makes the heavens and the earth do his bidding. "The plagues are a revelation," says Peter Enns. "They are not done in private, but for all the world to see. They tell us, in no uncertain terms, who God is and what he can do."[5] This is the meaning of the exodus story: God is sovereign. Not Moses. Not Pharaoh. God alone. The deliverance of Israel will be God's doing.

The Passover

We do not know what the Egyptians do to prepare for the night of the last plague, but we know exactly what the Hebrews are doing. The Israelites are undergoing an elaborate ritual that will serve to warn the death angel away from their dwellings.

This ritualized night becomes known as Passover, detailed in Exodus 12:1-28. The focus of Passover is the lamb. A firstborn lamb from the flock, a yearling free of disease or defect, is selected. The afternoon of the Passover, the head of each family slaughters the lamb at twilight and carefully collects the blood in a basin. The Jews are to dip flimsy hyssop plants into the basins of blood and apply the blood to the two side posts and lintels of their houses.[6] The blood will be a sign to the destroyer that the occupants of that house are placing themselves under God's protection. Because the firstborn lamb has died as a substitute, the firstborn Israelite is spared. The night comes to be called "Passover" because God will *pass over* the Israelite houses, thereby protecting them.

The Passover marks the birth of the nation of Israel. From this point on, the Hebrew people will celebrate Passover to mark the first month of the Jewish year. The ritual meal that takes place on the night of the tenth plague becomes a sacred observance that is repeated every year.

Israel will never forget the experience of Passover. When their children ask the meaning of the ceremony, they are to say, "It is the Passover sacrifice to the LORD, who passed over the houses of the Israelites in Egypt and spared our homes when he struck down the Egyptians" (Exodus 12:27). The Passover becomes an annual opportunity to reflect on the acts of God that called Israel into existence. As succeeding generations observe Passover, they remember God's marvelous work of deliverance.

Leadership Lesson: The power of ritual and memory is that they allow groups to affirm identity and remember God's creative acts of deliverance.

There are certain commemorations that are important to every organization. These occasions strengthen identity and commemorate special times in the history of a group. When the events being commemorated are related to God, they should include worship.

Two important God-given ceremonies, or sacraments, include baptism and Communion.

Jesus and Passover

The Gospel writers closely associate the Lord's crucifixion with the Passover. In the context of the Passover holiday, God performed his greatest act of deliverance by providing his Son as the spotless, perfect Lamb who delivered the whole world. The early church also saw Passover as prefiguring the death of Jesus. They spoke of Christ as "our Passover lamb" (1 Corinthians 5:7).

For Christians, Jesus Christ is the new Passover Lamb, and the Lord's Supper is the new Passover. Jesus, "a lamb without blemish or defect" (1 Peter 1:19), is led to Golgotha about noon—the exact time when the priests are slaughtering Passover lambs in the temple courts (between noon and sundown).[7] In this way, Jesus is ingeniously equated with the Passover lamb and his blood understood as redemptive.

Remember Isaac's question to Abraham? He asks, "Where is the lamb?" (Genesis 22:7). This question, a theme throughout the Old Testament, is ultimately answered by John the Baptist. He points to Jesus and proclaims, "Look, the Lamb of God, who takes away the sin of the world!" (John 1:29).

Questions for Leadership Development

1. What are the fruits of a heart that is soft and obedient?

2. What is the difference between planning and preparation? Is one more important than the other?

3. What rituals and commemorations are important to your organization?

ELEVEN

THE EXODUS:
THE FIRST FREEDOM MARCH

Let the fire and cloudy pillar
Lead me all my journey through;
Strong Deliverer, strong Deliverer,
Be thou still my Strength and Shield,
Be thou still my Strength and Shield.

William Williams[1]

The exodus from Egypt takes place the morning after the Passover meal. The Israelites march boldly out of Egypt in full view of their former oppressors, who are busy burying their dead (see Numbers 33:3–4). The Israelites are free.

Leadership Lesson: We serve a God who can—and will—deliver his people.

We have all been slaves in our own Egypt, in need of God's deliverance. None of us has the power to bring about deliverance from our personal bondage. If not for the goodness of the Lord, we would still be slaves to our own sinful condition. But, just as God acts decisively to bring about Israel's deliverance, he has also acted to bring about our deliverance through Jesus Christ. God continues to act to deliver his people. With a mighty hand and an outstretched arm, he brings us out of our bondage.

As Moses leads the children of Israel out of Goshen, the procession carries bones, battle gear, and baskets of dough. The bones belong to Joseph, and are taken to fulfill the promise made to him hundreds of years before (Exodus 13:19). The men carry weapons of war, most likely spears. The women shoulder kneading troughs and unleavened bread. Their departure is so sudden that they carry only a meager supply of dough, prepared in such haste that they do not bother to leaven it. Instead of baking loaves, they will roll out the dough into round cakes and bake them into *matzah*—the dry, cracker-like "bread of affliction" (Deuteronomy 16:3).

When Joseph brought his family to Egypt, there were about seventy in number. When Moses leads the Israelites out of Egypt, there are probably close to or more than two million.[2]

Leadership Lesson: God wants to take his people on a journey.

The role of the leader is to discern where God wants his people to go and how to get there. Faith is dynamic. We are meant to be a people on the move. We are not meant to stay mired in captivity. By faith, we can be sure there is meaning in our moving, even when it is not entirely clear to us. God is taking us on a journey.

Apparently, the Israelites are not the only people to leave Egypt at this time. According to Exodus 12:38, many other people take advantage of the devastated and demoralized Egyptian nation and escape with the Israelites.

Leadership Lesson: **The blessings of God are not limited to one people or group.**

When God acts to deliver—whether it be a person or a group—others benefit as well.

As Israel departs from Egypt, God goes before them to show them the way. The Hebrews are guided by a pillar of cloud by day that becomes a pillar of fire by night (Exodus 13:21). The pillar of cloud appears for the first time when the Hebrews leave Egypt. It goes ahead of them during the day to direct them in the way they should go. A visible manifestation of God's presence, the cloud is an encouraging reminder that they are not alone. The cloud is a pledge that God will be with his people to protect them.

The cloud also provides shade, protecting the people from the hot sun as they travel. At night, when they cannot see a cloud, God provides a pillar of fire within the cloud, which offers illumination and warmth as well as protection from wild animals. When the pillar, whether cloud or fire, moves the camp moves; when the pillar stops the camp stops (Exodus 40:36–37). Sometimes the cloud stays only from the evening to the morning. Sometimes it stays for three days, sometimes for a week, sometimes for a month, and sometimes for a year or longer.

Leadership Lesson: **God's guidance provides great comfort.**

The cloud that leads the Israelites is visible and unmistakable. Their direction and their speed are determined by the Lord. When God moves the people move. When God stays put so do they. God is their light. God is their shield. God is their guide. He shows them where to go and when.

While we don't have the same kind of visible guidance today, we do have both the Bible and the Holy Spirit. We have the assurance that God's word is "a lamp for my feet, a light on my path" (Psalm 119:105). We also have the Holy Spirit, who does not only dwell over us but also within us. The Spirit enables us to understand the Bible and to walk in the light it provides.

It is also noteworthy that the pillar of fire that gives light to the Jews casts darkness for the Egyptians (Exodus 14:20). When the Israelites seem to be trapped between the Red Sea and the Egyptian army, the cloud goes behind them and provides light in the camp of the Israelites and darkness in the camp of the Egyptians. The same light that brings illumination to one person can bring blindness to another.

Following the cloud, when the Hebrews leave Egypt they are not led in a direct route toward the promised land. The shortest route is to go up the coast into Philistine territory. The easiest route to Canaan lays through the Isthmus of Suez and the land of the Philistines. It is a journey of a little more than a hundred miles. But God does not permit them to go that way. Though that way is shorter and they are armed for battle, God does not take them through Philistine country.

The reason stated is that the shorter route will bring them into military conflict with the Philistines (13:17). That route will mean war, not only with the Philistines but also at Egyptian fortifications along the way. God's evaluation is that war might drive them back to Egypt, so they do not go that way. It is difficult to understand why God would have the Israelites avoid war now, only to see it happen two months later (17:8–16). Perhaps one reason is that the route Israel takes gives Egypt impulse to follow. Peter Enns says, "This alternate route will result in a much *greater* test of their faith (being hemmed in by the sea) than open conflict with the Philistines might."[3]

Leadership Lesson: Life seldom occurs in a straight line.

When God leads the Hebrews out of Egypt, he does not take them out via the highway or give them the most direct route to the promised pand. Rather, he leads them on the back roads, taking them along a longer route toward the Red Sea.

Detours through the wilderness are often designed to accomplish divine purposes. The shortest, quickest, or easiest way to a destination might not allow adequate time to develop the character that will be needed at the destination.

Questions for Leadership Development

1. Where are you leading the people you serve?

2. How has God delivered you?

3. In what ways do you find guidance from God?

TWELVE

THE RED SEA: GOD'S DELIVERANCE

When Israel out of bondage came,
A sea before them lay;
My Lord reached down his mighty hand,
And rolled the sea away.

Henry J. Zelley[1]

No sooner does Israel leave Egypt than Pharaoh begins to regret that he has let them go. The forfeiture of the slave force is more than he can endure. With the departure of the Hebrews, Egypt has lost its primary source of manpower and much of the private wealth of the nation.

When three days lapse and the Israelites are not turning back toward Egypt, Pharaoh resolves to put an end to the Israelite insurrection once and for all. Egypt's best troops are outfitted with Egypt's finest chariots and sent to bring the Hebrews back.

As the Israelites journey from Egypt, they make their way into an area in which they can be easily trapped. There is sand on one side, mountains on the other, and a sea in front of them. It seems as though the tactic of setting up camp with their backs against the sea is an invitation to disaster. The maneuver puts the

Israelites at the mercy of an attacking army and cuts off any line of escape. They are literally caught between the Pharaoh and the Red Sea. There is no apparent way out except the way they came.

Leadership Lesson: **God's children sometimes find themselves in places of profound difficulty.**

The question becomes, how will you respond? Will you allow God's record of faithfulness and his good promises to give you hope, or will you abandon hope and despair of life? Good leaders have the opportunity to encourage demoralized followers and point them to the God of hope.

Though the Israelites march out of Egypt boldly, when they see the Egyptian horses, chariots, and troops marching after them, they lose heart and cry out in terror. One glimpse of the Egyptian army throws the Israelites into panic. They fear being massacred in the desert. Their response to their predicament is terror, accusation, and criticism of what they judge to be Moses's failed leadership. "Was it because there were no graves in Egypt that you brought us to the desert to die? What have you done to us by bringing us out of Egypt? Didn't we say to you in Egypt, 'Leave us alone; let us serve the Egyptians'? It would have been better for us to serve the Egyptians than to die in the desert!" (Exodus 14:11-12).

Jonathan Kirsch says, "Four centuries of slavery had tainted the souls of the Israelites, weakened their will, and left them cowardly, cynical, and calculating. The Israelites were armed, but they dared not fight, even though they vastly outnumbered the Egyptians. After all, six hundred thousand men-at-arms ought to have been able to repulse six hundred chariots. Instead they complained about the peril into which Moses had led them."[2]

Leadership Lesson: When it seems you are hemmed in and you do not know which way to turn, turn to God.

In Exodus 14:13–14, Moses tells the Hebrews exactly what to do in times of fear and great stress: 1) fear not, 2) stand still, 3) see what God will do, and 4) stay silent while the Lord fights for you. This is exactly opposite of the typical human response to crisis, which is: 1) become fearful, 2) run, 3) fight on your own, and 4) tell everybody but God your predicament.[3]

When it appears the enemy has you hemmed in, remember that God has you surrounded. The psalmist declares, "You hem me in behind and before, and you lay your hand upon me" (139:5). We are instructed to wait and see the deliverance of the Lord. Fear of the enemy leads to despair, while trust in God leads to hope. Trying situations become opportunities to place trust in God and see his deliverance.

Moses has confidence in God's ability to save. He tells the Israelites to not be afraid, and he assures them that they will see the Lord's deliverance. The Lord then instructs Moses to tell the Israelites to march forward. Moses is to raise his staff and stretch his hand out over the sea so the water will be divided and the Israelites can cross on dry ground, with walls of water on their right and on their left.

All night long, the Lord sends a strong east wind that drives the sea back and turns it into dry land (Exodus 14:21). At the same time, the angel of God and the pillar of cloud, both of which have been in front of the Israelites, move around behind them, between the Egyptians and the Hebrews, shielding the Israelites from their attackers. The pillar gives light to Israel but darkness to the enemy. God becomes a wall of protection between his people and their enemies.

Leadership Lesson: However difficult your predicament, however threatening the situation, God can make a way.

When you are stuck between a rock and a hard place, take courage in the fact that God can deliver people who cannot deliver themselves. He can make a way.

As soon as the Egyptians see that Israel is escaping, they follow the Israelites into the sea. As the Egyptians pursue the Israelites across the sea, the army is thrown into confusion. In addition, the chariots malfunction so they have difficulty driving. The Egyptians quickly lose their will to fight. But before they can retreat, Moses once again stretches his hand out over the sea from the far shore, and the sea returns to its place. The Egyptians are overwhelmed by the sudden rush of water toppling down on them from either side and are swept into the sea. There are no survivors—Pharaoh's entire army is lost.

The military might of the Egyptians is shattered. That which the Israelites feared most has been rendered powerless. And, in an ironic twist, in the same way Pharaoh destroyed the Jewish babies by drowning them, so God now destroys Pharaoh's army by drowning.

An amazing scene takes place the next morning on the shore of the Red Sea. As the sun comes up, the Israelites see the bodies of their enemies washed up on the shore. A song of deliverance swells from their ranks, led by Moses and his sister, Miriam (Exodus 15:1–21).

In honor of God's dramatic victory over the Egyptian army at the Red Sea, the Israelites sing, celebrating their new freedom. There is no thought of anyone but the Lord in this song. Moses is referred to not once. God, and only God, is glorified. The stated purpose of this hymn, from the beginning, is to exalt God. The song moves from a celebration of God's deliverance to the victories that are to come.

Miriam provides the benediction, proclaiming, "Sing to the LORD, for he is highly exalted. Both horse and driver he has hurled into the sea" (v. 21).

Leadership Lesson: Music provides a wonderful way to celebrate deliverance.

After God-given victories there should always be a song to God. Moses's song of praise serves as an example of a song that focuses exclusively on God and what God has done. At the Red Sea, God puts gladness in their hearts and a new song in their mouths. We serve the God who can turn our fretful anxieties into songs of praise.

What happens at the Red Sea will never be forgotten by Israel. The crossing of the Red Sea is mentioned more in the Old Testament than the Passover. For generations to come, the judges, poets, and prophets of Israel will write of the deliverance of Israel at the Red Sea. The moment is seared into their collective memory. Israel has discovered how God leads, protects, and delivers his people. This deliverance apparently also becomes known among the other nations because, when the Israelites come to conquer the promised land and the two Hebrew spies make their way to Jericho, Rahab the prostitute tells them, "We have heard how the LORD dried up the water of the Red Sea for you when you came out of Egypt" (Joshua 2:10).

Charles Swindoll says, "The crossing of the Red Sea is to the Old Testament what the resurrection is to the New. When the prophets and writers of the Old Testament wanted to refer to God's miraculous hand, they returned to this event more than any other. Just so, when a writer in the New Testament wanted to illustrate the power of God, he most often referred to the resurrection."[4]

Israel will once again put their trust in the Lord and in Moses. Their trust, however, is short-lived.

Questions for Leadership Development

1. When you find yourself in a place of profound difficulty, how do you usually respond?

2. When God acts in a significant way to bless you or the people you serve, how do you celebrate that event?

— THIRTEEN —

MARAH:
LIFE'S BITTER PLACES

When the root is bitterness,
imagine what the fruit might be.
Woodrow Kroll[1]

After leaving the Red Sea, the Israelites travel three days in the desert without locating water. When they do find water, they can't drink it because it is bitter. Their relief at discovering water turns to disappointment when it is undrinkable. The Israelites find it difficult to believe that the God who so recently led them through the Red Sea will also deliver them from their present trouble. As is often the case when disappointment and discontent marry, bitterness is the product.

The propensity of the Israelites to grumble and murmur and bitterly complain can be seen as early as Exodus 5:21, when they condemn Moses for Pharaoh's actions. Resentful, grumbling, and hostile speech marks the Israelites' forty-year sojourn in the wilderness. One would think God's deliverance of the Israelites from the Egyptian army would result in optimistic attitudes and buoyed faith. However, within three days of seeing the greatest deliverance recorded in the Old Testament, the children of Israel are again bitterly complaining. While it appears that Moses's trust in God's faithfulness continues to grow, the same is apparently not true for the Israelites.

Exodus 15:22–17:7 contains three stories that deal with the Israelites' grumbling over a lack of water and food: water at Marah (15:22-27); manna and quail (16:1-36); and lack of water at Rephidim (17:1-7). The first of these insurrection stories begins with the water at Marah.

As the Israelites start out from the Red Sea, their hearts are cheerful. They have just seen God's wonderful deliverance. They have the pillar of fire and cloud to assure them of God's presence and protection.

But as they travel south through the wilderness, they find no wells, no oases, no sources of water for them or their flocks. The goatskins that were filled with water at the Red Sea run dry after only three days. The problem of too much water at the Red Sea is followed by the problem of too little water in the desert. By the third day the people are thirsty. Mouths are parched and dry. Tongues are thick like sandpaper. Discontent is rising. Warren Wiersbe says, "A single day in the wilderness without water would be tolerable, two days would be difficult, but three days would be impossible, especially for children and animals."[2]

Finally, they reach Marah. When they arrive at that spring, they probably rush headlong to the water, only to discover that the water is bitter and makes them nauseated. The people cannot drink it. They name the spring Marah, which means "bitter" in Hebrew. The disappointment of the Israelites is evident: "So the people grumbled against Moses" (15:24).

Leadership Lesson: **Bitter places often result in bitter attitudes and bitter words.**

This is especially true of the Israelites. Bitter complaining is their default reaction to hard times. Jonathan Kirsch says, "Bitterness was the response of the Israelites to every moment of adversity and uncertainty in the wilderness, and Moses was always the target of their complaints."[3]

Disappointment and bitterness often go hand in hand. Dealing with disappointment can be a significant challenge in leadership, whether it's your own disappointment or the disappointment of those you serve.

Leaders should be aware of the destructive influence of unrealized expectations, which can often lead to disappointment and bitterness. Giving people an opportunity to express their expectations can sometimes help them recognize when those expectations are unrealistic. Communication—especially communication that shapes expectations—becomes integral to leadership when groups find themselves in disappointing circumstances.

Often, a journey will bring you to places filled with disappointment, unmet expectations, or extreme difficulty. The attitude that marks your conduct when bitter things come your way will likely determine the effectiveness of your leadership in troubling times. Bitter places need not translate into bitter attitudes, words, or hearts. All leaders will find themselves at Marah at some point in their leadership journeys. Disappointments will come, but places of disappointment don't have to become places of bitterness.

At Marah, Moses realizes he is in trouble, and he does what good leaders do when they find themselves in trouble. Moses turns to God in prayer. He cries out to God, who instructs Moses to take a piece of wood and throw it into the water. When he does so, the water becomes drinkable (v. 25).[4]

Leadership Lesson: When in trouble, turn to God.

God permits the Marahs in our life not only to test our faith but also to prove his faithfulness. He uses those experiences to reveal what is in us and then provides us the opportunity to experience his provision. The God who led you through your own Red Sea experience—whether recently or long ago—will also deliver you from your present trouble.

The Israelites are disappointed at Marah, but they are surprised and delighted when the journey next leads them to Elim. There they discover twelve springs of water providing the sweet, cool refreshment they have longed for. It is possible that each tribe drank from its own spring. There are also seventy palm trees that provide shade and an opportunity for rest and relaxation. Elim represents a place of healing and restoration.

Leadership Lesson: Along the journey you will experience Marah, but you will also experience Elim.

Elim is a place that represents rest after a long desert march. Difficult circumstances provide God's people with opportunities to trust him in deeper ways than they have in the past, and to experience God's provision in new and refreshing ways. Usually the only way to Elim is through the desert, which makes the palm trees more beautiful, their shade more refreshing. The desert experience makes the well water cooler and more invigorating. Those places of refreshment and relaxation help us recover from the difficult seasons of life and prepare us for the next stretch of the journey.

Questions for Leadership Development

1. How do you deal with personal disappointment before it leads to bitterness?

2. To what degree can providing communication and managing expectations diminish the potential disappointment of those you serve?

3. Where is your Elim, your place of refreshment?

— FOURTEEN —

MANNA AND QUAIL: GIVE US THIS DAY

Guide me, O thou great Jehovah,
Pilgrim through this barren land;
I am weak, but thou art mighty;
Hold me with thy pow'rful hand;
Bread of heaven, Bread of heaven,
Feed me 'til I want no more,
Feed me 'til I want no more.

William Williams[1]

Exodus 16 begins with "the whole community" grumbling against Moses and Aaron (v. 1). They have just seen the deliverance of the Lord at the Red Sea, experienced the waters of Marah made drinkable, and enjoyed the shade, beauty, and refreshment of the oasis at Elim.

But once their stomachs began to rumble, their mouths began to grumble. They miss the "fleshpots" of Egypt (v. 3, NRSV). An angry mob accuses Moses and Aaron of leading Israel into the desert to starve them to death when they could have sat around pots of meat and eaten all the food they wanted in Egypt. Moses finds the complaint exasperating. Meat was a rarity among the slaves in ancient Egypt, and "the good old days" are being remembered as better than they actually were. "We sat around pots of meat" (v. 3) is an exaggeration—something the discontent are given to. The Israelites are twisting the facts in order to build a stronger case against their leader. Life in Egypt was not one long barbecue buffet line. They are exaggerating the meager provisions they had in Egypt and diminishing the resources they presently have in the desert.

In response to the complaints of the Israelites over their hunger, the Lord tells Moses to expect "bread from heaven" to begin to fall like rain each day (v. 4). The people are able to gather enough to meet their need for daily bread.

The word "manna" comes from the question the Jews ask the first morning the bread appears. The people are surprised at the appearance of the bread, and their initial response is to ask, "What is it?" or *man hu* in Hebrew (v. 15). The question the Israelites ask becomes the name of the nourishment—manna, bread of heaven.

God gives specific instructions related to the manna. Six mornings a week everyone is to gather as much as required for their needs and the needs of their family. On average, each person will gather an omer (about three pounds). The manna is to be eaten that day, not kept overnight. Those who do keep it overnight will find it full of maggots and foul-smelling the next morning. On the sixth day they are to gather enough for two days because none will be provided on the Sabbath. Heaven's kitchen is idle on the seventh day.

The manna comes down with the dew each night. In the morning, when the layer of dew on the ground dries, thin flakes like frost appear on the desert floor. The delicious, delicate treat is white like coriander seed, looks like resin, and tastes like wafers made with honey and olive oil. The promised land is described as a land of milk and honey, and this manna serves as an appetizer, a foretaste of the blessings of Canaan.

Leadership Lesson: We only need bread for today.

The daily meal in the wilderness is evidence of God's provision. It cannot be taken for granted, and it cannot be hoarded. They must trust God each morning to supply what they need for that day. Manna becomes a daily reminder to Israel and to us that God is the source of life. God will provide for each person exactly what they need in their particular situation. The food is not to be hoarded, but God is to be trusted anew each day. Israel is kept in a perpetual state of dependence.

Jesus encourages us to pray for "daily bread" (Matthew 6:11; Luke 11:3). This is how we learn to trust God daily. We find our security in God, who each day proves himself to be faithful. We must be willing to receive provision from his hand day by day.

The Gospel writers present Jesus as the true Bread of heaven who gives eternal life to those who believe in him. In John 6:22–59, the day after Jesus fed more than five thousand people with five barley loaves and two small fish, he preaches a sermon about the bread of life to a crowd in the synagogue at Capernaum. Jesus declares that he is "the true bread" (v. 32) that has come down from heaven for hungry sinners.

Soldiers in every age have complained about their rations, and so does the army that marches behind Moses. They soon grow tired of manna and want meat. After breaking camp at Sinai, the Israelites begin to complain about the food God is providing. This time they complain not about the lack of food but about the lack of variety.

Leadership Lesson: "Grumblers gonna grumble."

Charles Swindoll says grumbling can become the standard response of those who are perpetually dissatisfied. "That's the way grumblers are. They gripe when they don't have it, but when they get it, they gripe because it isn't their preferred variety. And when they get their preferred variety, they gripe because they'd rather try something else."[2]

The Israelites do not like the food they are given. They grow tired of the daily fare of manna, and they crave meat. So God sends quail. God tells Moses to tell the people that if they want meat, God will give them meat. In fact, they will have so much meat that it cannot be consumed in a day, or even in a week. They will eat meat for an entire month, "until it comes out of your nostrils and you loathe it" (Numbers 11:20).

That night, a wind drives the quail in from the sea and scatters them in heaps up to three feet tall all around the camp. A Hebrew can walk for an entire day from the center of the camp, in any direction, and still see heaps of quail. For the next two days, the people gather quail.

The manna and quail are supernatural gifts. God provides them. However, the Israelites do have to work to gather it. "Manna did not fall into the Israelites' mouths," says James Boice. "They had to go out in the morning and gather it up."[3]

Leadership Lesson: There is a correlation between divine provision and human responsibility.

God seldom does everything himself. God expects human participation to accompany his divine provision. God supplies the manna, but the Israelites must harvest it, pick it up, prepare it, and eat it. God will provide the quail, but the Israelites must gather it, clean it, cook it, and eat it. God will provide victory over the enemy, but Israel must take up arms and participate. As one theologian puts it, "Divine purpose and human responsibility dance with each other."[4]

God has now done two things to miraculously provide food for the people. First, he provides manna, the bread-like substance they find on the ground in the mornings. Second, he provides quail. God will not only provide food and water for the journey but clothing as well. As Scripture says, the clothes of the Israelites do not wear out for forty years. Nor do their feet swell (Deuteronomy 8:4).

Manna is supernatural food only given to the Israelites during the wilderness wanderings. The manna stops the day the Israelites arrive in Canaan and gain access to the produce of the land (Exodus 16:35; Joshua 5:11–12).[8]

In time, a jar filled with manna will be placed in the ark of the covenant as a memorial to the way God provided for his children as they traveled the wilderness (Exodus 16:33; Hebrews 9:4). The jar will serve as a perpetual reminder, lest God's people forget the story of their deliverance and his provision.

Questions for Leadership Development

1. As a leader, how do you help grumblers realize that their default setting might need to be reset?

2. In what ways do you trust God for daily provision?

3. What is the correlation between divine provision and human responsibility in your own life?

— FIFTEEN —

AMALEKITES: ANCIENT TERRORISTS

There are three types of people in this world:
sheep, wolves, and sheepdogs.
Wayne Kyle[1]

The Sinai Peninsula is a dangerous place. In Moses's day, nomadic tribes that ranged the wilderness were quick to do battle with any group who entered their territory. Before the Israelites reach Mount Sinai, they battle one of those tribes, the Amalekites, who will become their perennial enemies.

The Amalekites are a vicious, fighting people who descend from Esau's grandson, Amalek (see Genesis 36:12). They are fierce nomads who roam the territory, raiding anybody who tries to pass through. Their usual strategy is cowardly, picking off stragglers at the end of a column—people who are famished, powerless, weary, old, sick, and cannot keep up with the main caravan. In Deuteronomy 25:17–18, Moses recalls the barbaric, vile tactics of the Amalekites, who attack Israel suddenly from behind in order to prey on the weakest.

The Amalekites are the terrorists of the ancient world. They are the first people to attack as the Israelites make their way toward the promised land, launching a surprise assault, unprovoked and unannounced. The evil deed is compounded by the fact that they target the feeble and elderly.

Leadership Lesson: **Leaders act to protect those they serve.**

When wolves threaten the flock, the shepherd must guard against, and sometimes do battle with, such threats. Leaders have a responsibility to protect their community. They must be willing to confront wolves and other predators who prey on the weak, the unempowered, and the helpless.

In a short span of time, Israel experiences miraculous deliverance at the Red Sea, the supernatural provision of manna and quail, an extraordinary provision of water at Marah, and a wonderful season of refreshment at Elim. The Amalekite attack comes on the heels of these great blessings.

Leadership Lesson: **The enemy often attacks God's people after they've experienced special blessings, in order to stop momentum.**

The Amalekite attack is designed to reverse the progress the Israelites are making in the journey. It is not unusual for the enemy to attack after a time of great victory. For example, in 1 Kings 18 we read that Elijah becomes discouraged and is tempted to quit *after* he defeats the priests of Baal (18:41–19:18). Jesus is tempted by the devil in the wilderness *after* his baptism (Matthew 3:13–4:1). The enemy desires to stop your momentum and reverse your forward progress. After seasons of significant progress, don't be surprised if you experience an attack by the enemy.

When the Amalekites attack Israel at Rephidim, Moses appoints Joshua, a man about half his age, to be commander of the troops (Exodus 17:9).

The Israelites have weapons in hand that they have carried out of Egypt, but they have no combat experience. Nor does their leader, Joshua, have experience leading an army. It is remarkable that in this first encounter with an armed enemy, the Israelites are disciplined, engaging the enemy without breaking and running. The slaves become soldiers and win their first battle. And the victory comes about in an amazing way.

The story of the battle is found in Exodus 17. Moses, Aaron, and Hur strategically place themselves on the top of a hill, where they have a commanding view of the battle taking place below. Moses's staff is in his hands. As long as Moses holds up his hands and his staff, Joshua and the Israelites are winning the battle. But when Moses's arms grow tired and the staff lowers, the Amalekites begin to win the battle.

So Aaron and Hur find a rock for Moses to sit on. They hold Moses's hands up until the sun sets, and Joshua and the Israelites defeat the Amalekites. This is a marvelous picture of friends standing together in intercession for the people of God.

Leadership Lesson: Don't underestimate the power of prayer when it comes to winning battles.

As is true in so many of life's battles, unless the Lord intervenes, the battle is lost. This is a lesson Israel needs to learn. Moses's raised hands "do not merely provide psychological support but rather unleash divine power."[2]

Just as the victory over the Amalekites is dependent upon the Lord, so are the rest of the battles Israel will face—on both sides of the Jordan. The nations on the other side of the river will be more powerful than Israel has the ability to overcome without divine help.

We are often not capable in ourselves to be victorious. But "the one who is in [us] is greater than the one who is in the world" (1 John 4:4).

So memorable is the victory over the Amalekites at Rephidim that Moses pauses to build an altar called Adonai Nissi, "The LORD is my banner" (Exodus 17:15).

Because of the cowardly and brutal way in which the Amalekites act toward the Israelites, the Lord declares to Moses that Israel should contend with Amalek until that nation is completely destroyed (vv. 14–16). In Deuteronomy 25:19, Moses summons a new generation of Israelites to blot out the memory of the Amalekites. The descendants of Amalek are to have no future.

In the future, Israel, Gideon, Saul, and David will all contend with the Amalekites (see Numbers 14:45; Judges 6:33; 1 Samuel 15; 30; 2 Samuel 1:1–16; 8:11–12). The Amalekites will finally be annihilated during the reign of Hezekiah (1 Chronicles 4:41–43). The Amalekites are only the first of a long line of enemies whom the Israelites will engage in battle.

Leadership Lesson: Future generations will need to finish some of the battles we start.[3]

Just as succeeding generations continued to battle against the Amalekites, we may not be able to finish the fight against human trafficking, world hunger, or any other threat that preys on the weakest among us. Still, it's important we get the fight started.

Questions for Leadership Development

1. To what degree should leaders protect those they serve? Are there limits to the protection? If so, what are those limits?

2. Has there been a time in your life when a leader interceded for you? If so, what were the circumstances, and how did you feel?

3. If you were to construct an altar to commemorate a recent victory, what would you name that altar?

— SIXTEEN —

JETHRO: ONE REASON LEADERS CRACK UP

Fools are headstrong and do what they like;
wise people take advice.
Proverbs 12:15 (MSG)

There is an air of mystery around Jethro, Moses's father-in-law, due in part to some confusion about his name.[1] We know very little about him, other than he has daughters and flocks, and that he is a priest of Midian (Exodus 2:16; 18:1). As a Midianite, we know he is a descendent of Abraham (see Genesis 25:1–2).[2] His name means "friend of God" or "God is my shepherd."[3]

Moses seems to have a great relationship with his father-in-law. After his encounter with God at the burning bush, Moses returns to Jethro to ask permission to return to Egypt (Exodus 4:18), and apparently to return Jethro's sheep. This show of deference is Moses's acknowledgement of Jethro's status as his elder. After telling Jethro he wants to visit Egypt to see if his family is alive, Moses receives Jethro's blessing.

Some time passes, and, having heard back in Midian of all that God has done for Moses and the Israelites in delivering them from Egypt, Jethro decides to journey out into the wilderness of Sinai in search of his son-in-law. He also brings Moses's wife, Zipporah, and their two sons, Gershom and Eliezer.

When Jethro appears at the camp of the Israelites, Moses gives him a royal welcome with a great show of respect and affection. Moses tells Jethro all the things God has done on behalf of the people—the plagues and the Passover, the Red Sea deliverance, and the victory over the Amalekites. Obviously impressed with what God has done for the children of Israel, Jethro offers a sacrifice (Exodus 18:12).

Moses is at a breaking point when his father-in-law's timely visit occurs, encumbered with the overwhelming responsibilities of leading the Hebrew children out of Egypt and toward the promised land. Exodus 18 gives us a glimpse into the kind of life Moses is leading. When the Hebrews set up camp and there is a day of liberty from the weariness of the march, Moses sits on a judgment seat. All the people come to him who have any dispute or grievance or matters about which they desire counsel or judgment. When approximately two million people are living and traveling together, there are bound to be disputes. At this point in the journey, Moses is the sole mediator.

Leadership Lesson: Leaders will always have to deal with conflict management, managing both their own conflicts as well as conflicts between those they lead.

As long as there are people living in community, there will be conflict. This is true in homes, in neighborhoods, in churches, in businesses, in schools, and in every organization. Skills in conflict management and relational intelligence are critical to leadership.

Jethro observes the style and nature of Moses's leadership first-hand. He sees how the people come to Moses from morning to night. Moses is doing too much on his own and has neglected to ask others to help shoulder the load. Although the nation already has elders (Exodus 4:29), they are apparently not assisting Moses in the day-to-day activities of the camp.

Jethro sees this taking place and tells Moses, "What you are doing is not good. You and these people who come to you will only wear yourselves out. The work is too heavy for you; you cannot handle it alone" (18:17–18).

Leadership Lesson: Leaders do not always realize the personal toll of leadership.

F. B. Meyer says, "We do not always see the cost at which we are doing our work. We are sustained by the excitement and interest of it."[4] For many leaders, it feels like there is always one more thing to be done. The organizations we serve may never say, "You've done enough; please rest." Rather, we may always be expected to do just a little bit more. As the burdens and responsibilities compound, reserves are soon expended.

It would be nice if we had easy-to-read gauges that assessed how much fuel was left in our tanks. But often we find ourselves suddenly depleted. Fortunately for Moses, he had a friend who was able to speak into his situation.

Jethro's words "wear yourselves out" (v. 18) come from a Hebrew term that means "to be withered with exhaustion" or "to sink or drop down, languish, wither, and fall."[5] Carrying people and their burdens taxes the sympathies, drains the brain, and wearies the heart. Caring for the needs of troubled souls can sap your strength over time—especially if it is kept up without respite.

Jethro observes what is happening to Moses and offers sound advice: get some help. He warns Moses that he will be unable to sustain his current pace.

Leadership Lesson: There can be great value in having someone (a coach, consultant, or trusted advisor) observe and evaluate your leadership style and effectiveness.

Up to this time, Moses has taken all his instructions directly from God. Now, God provides wisdom to Moses through Jethro. The wise leader is open to wise counsel. Be willing to listen to trusted counselors and people of wisdom whom God wants to use to speak truth into your life.

Jethro, who has become Moses's efficiency expert, asks two questions: 1) What are you doing? (a question of priorities), and 2) Why are you doing it all alone? (a question of personnel resources).[6]

Jethro observes that not only is Moses's leadership approach overtaxing him but it is also allowing a large amount of talent to go unused. He offers some fatherly advice, counseling Moses to divide the labor by shifting some of the burden to trusted subordinates.

Jethro suggests that Moses select capable men to act as judges over an assigned group of people for the simple cases. Moses will concern himself with only the difficult cases (18:21–22). Moses is to organize the camp so that every ten people have somebody to talk to about their civil problems. If the leader of ten cannot resolve the issue, it will be taken to the leader of fifty, then one hundred, then one thousand. Lastly, it will be referred to Moses himself.

Leadership Lesson: **Delegation—the assigning of responsibility to others—makes a team stronger.**

Jethro makes it clear that Moses must build a team. He suggests that Moses identify, recruit, and develop leaders who can share in the responsibility. In fact, he suggests that the team not only help Moses but also mentor others to be leaders. Jethro understands the importance of developing a leadership team and knows the best way to do this is to create a leadership pipeline—a process by which leaders are both being mentored and mentoring others at the same time. Building a strong team helps address current needs. It also sets the stage for a strong future.

Jethro gives Moses three qualifications for appointed judges: 1) They must be individuals who "fear God." This means their leadership will be based on wisdom and godly, spiritual maturity. 2) They must love truth and be trustworthy. This means they are worthy of trust, capable, have the ability to think clearly, can objectively weigh evidence, and be fair. 3) They must hate dishonest gain. This means they have financial integrity, are in it for the people and not the money, refuse corrupt personal benefit, and anticipate—and reject—bribery (18:21).

Leadership Lesson: **When building a team, it is necessary to keep in mind the qualities for good leadership.**

Jethro gives Moses good advice: "select capable individuals." Moses does this by asking the Israelite people to select candidates they know are qualified. Moses appoints, but only after the people nominate individuals they know are able to handle their cases.

In Exodus 18:20–22, Jethro gives Moses four steps to follow in implementation:

1) Choose the right people—those who meet the qualifications of being spiritually mature, trustworthy, and impartial. The important thing about delegating responsibilities is that you have leaders who have ability as well as credibility, competence, and character.

2) Train the people well. Moses is to teach Israel the decrees and instructions of the Lord, showing them how to live in ways that honor God and their fellow Israelites. This step alone will reduce the number of legal cases.

3) Empower and authorize the leaders in front of the people they will be leading.

4) Make clear to the leaders what needs approval and what they can decide on their own.

Jethro further tells Moses that his priorities should be giving himself to prayer and teaching the people the ways of God. If this counsel sounds familiar, it may be because the same thing takes place in Acts 6:1–7. The twelve disciples appoint seven men to oversee the distribution of resources so they can focus their attention on "prayer and the ministry of the word" (v. 4). The tasks of praying and teaching are exactly those given to ministers today.

Leadership Lesson: No one can do it all.

No one person possesses every gift. An individual may have several gifts, but nobody has all gifts. Even if a single person did have all the gifts, they would not have the time or strength needed to do everything that needs to be done. Not even Moses is up to that challenge.

Junia Pokrifka says, "God's purpose is to distribute gifts of ministry among all the people of God rather than having them permanently concentrated in one leader or a few leaders."[7] Delegating and sharing responsibility is critical in leadership. Moses is willing to acknowledge diverse gifts and distribute leadership functions.

Self-aware leaders realize at some point the necessity of letting go of certain responsibilities. Not only is it impossible to get to everything, but it is also impossible to be good at everything. Raising up new leaders is a good strategy for getting more done, and done better. Letting go of responsibilities others have been trained to pick up relieves your stress and increases their fulfillment.

Moses proceeds to implement a program by which certain tasks—particularly those of rendering judgments—are divided among designated leaders of the twelve tribes. Warren Wiersbe says, "According to Deuteronomy 1:9–18, Moses shared Jethro's counsel with the people, admitted his own weakness and weariness, and asked them to select leaders to assist him. They approved of the plan and selected the officers whom Moses then charged with the responsibilities of their offices."[8]

Leadership Lesson: Delegation can be achieved well when these four steps are followed.

First, determine what can be delegated. In Moses's case, routine, daily verdicts can be delegated. What are you doing that can and should be done by someone else?

Second, match tasks with gifts. Knowing the gift mix and strengths of your team is critical to delegating well.

Third, clarify expectations and provide training. Clearly define the assignment. There is a huge difference between dumping work on others and delegating effectively; that difference is training. Jethro tells Moses to communicate to the people, to "teach them [God's] decrees and instructions and show them the way they are to live and how they are to behave" (Exodus 18:20). Jethro is suggesting that Moses instruct the people as a whole so they understand God's expectations. Moses, up until that time, has been waiting for a problem to arise before sharing insights from God.

Fourth, regularly assess and affirm your leaders. Your responsibilities are not over once your tasks have been delegated. You still need to assess the effectiveness of the team and offer feedback and affirmation.

As already mentioned, Moses's leadership approach is adopted by the apostles when the business of the church grows beyond their scope. They can no longer do everything, so they call in the help of Stephen and his colleagues to serve tables while they give themselves to prayer and the ministry of the Word (Acts 6:1–7). These assistants must have good reputations, be full of the Spirit and wisdom, and approved by the people.

Leadership Lesson: **When delegation is not taking place, it is usually due to one of the following barriers:**

1) **Not enough time.** Sometimes leaders believe they do not have enough time to adequately explain a task or teach a skill. Training is time-consuming and messy, but there are high rewards. If you delegate, eventually you will have even more time to invest in more people.

2) **Insecurity**. Some leaders believe that the more they do, the more valuable they are. They fear losing prominence if others begin doing what the leader has been doing. They think their worth is based on what they personally produce. That is a works-based ministry philosophy, and it is neither effective nor biblical.

3) **Not understanding the value of equipping others**. When Paul provides a pastor's job description in Ephesians 4, he says pastors (and others) are to "equip [God's] people for works of service, so that the body of Christ may be built up" (v. 12). When leaders choose to play the role of every part of the body, they deny a fundamental truth that the body is many parts. If it seems there is no one to delegate to, pray that God will help you identify potential leaders. Then invest in them so they can become effective, responsible leaders themselves.

4) **Unrealistic expectations**. In some churches, pastors have borne the brunt of the work for so long that the congregation may see delegation as a shirking of responsibility, saying, "We pay the pastor to do that." Church leaders must have the courage and the patience to change that mindset through biblical teaching and effective training.[9]

Questions for Leadership Development

1. To what degree does your leadership responsibility involve conflict management? How might you become more effective in this area?

2. Who regularly speaks into your life with counsel and advice? Do you intentionally seek out such people?

3. How can you best guard against depleting your spiritual, relational, physical, or emotional reserves?

4. How would the people you serve assess your delegation skills?

5. Why do some leaders have difficulty recognizing their weaknesses and weariness?

6. What keeps you from delegating more than you presently do?

SEVENTEEN

MOUNT SINAI: THE PLACE WHERE LEADERS MEET GOD

The LORD would speak to Moses face to face,
as one speaks to a friend.
Exodus 33:11

Moses will climb several mountains over the course of his lifetime. The leader of Israel will trudge up Horeb, Sinai, Pisgah, and Nebo. But no mountain is more significant than Sinai, a mountain Moses climbs several times.

After the miracle of deliverance at the Red Sea, Moses begins the journey back to Mount Sinai, where he first encountered God. The 190-mile journey will take three months. Once the Israelites arrive, they will pitch their tents at the foot of the mountain for the next eleven months.

Sinai is a place of significant meaning for Moses. According to tradition, it is where he met his wife, Zipporah, forty years earlier. It is also where, mere months before leading the Israelites back to this place, Moses first encountered God when he heard his voice speak to him from the burning bush.

When God speaks to Moses from the burning bush, he gives Moses an encouraging promise: "I will be with you. And this will be the sign to you that it is I who have sent you: When you have brought the people out of Egypt, you will worship God on this mountain" (Exodus 3:12).

This promise is fulfilled when the Israelites arrive at "the mount of God." Fifty-nine chapters, from Exodus 19 to Numbers 10, will be devoted to their experience at Mount Sinai. Here, Moses will receive the Law, the tabernacle and its furnishings will be constructed, the priesthood will be established, the people will be numbered, and the tribes will be organized for their march to Kadesh-Barnea.

On the morning of the third day after the Israelites' arrival at Sinai, just as God told Moses and Moses told the people, the camp is suddenly awakened by strange sights and fearsome sounds. Thunder causes the mountain to tremble violently, and lightning flashes across its peak. The summit is covered by a thick cloud, and the sound of the ram's horn grows in intensity until they not only hear it with their ears but also feel it in their bones. As the Israelites creep out of their tents, they look up to see smoke billowing from the mountain "like smoke from a furnace" (Exodus 19:18). "The cloud and darkness, the thunder and lightning, the earthquake and fire," Warren Wiersbe says, "all manifested the fearsome greatness of God and produced a holy fear in the hearts of the people."[1] At Mount Sinai, a healthy fear and deep respect for the Almighty will be established.

Leadership Lesson: An awareness of the majesty of God is an awe-inspiring experience.

At Sinai the Israelites will learn of the majesty of God and that approaching God is a serious matter. Even the Israelites, God's own special possession, cannot simply sashay into his presence. God makes his presence known at Sinai in a way that is powerful and frightening.

For a people who regularly sing, "I am a friend of God," this passage reminds us of God's overwhelming Otherness. God's awesome majesty and dreadful splendor compel deep reverence and frightful awe.

For the Israelites, staying away from Mount Sinai is a matter of life or death. The presence of God sanctifies and sets apart the mountain (see Exodus 19:12–13, 20–25). Moses puts up barriers to keep the people at a distance and posts guards with authority to kill anybody who breaks through the barriers. "Keep your distance!" is Moses's emphasis. This same emphasis will mark the tabernacle after its construction. The fence around the tabernacle, the veil before the holy of holies, the fact that only the priests can minister in the tabernacle and only the high priest can enter the holy of holies, and that but once a year, will all remind the Israelites of God's holy Otherness.

In fact, it's possible Mount Sinai provides the basic blueprint for both the future tabernacle and temple.[2] Mount Sinai has three zones (foot, main mountain, top of the mountain) that correspond to the three areas of the tabernacle (courtyard, holy place, most holy place). The people are allowed access to the foot of the mountain and the courtyard. Only select leaders are permitted to enter the mountain or the holy place. And only one mediator (either Moses or a high priest) can enter the summit of the mountain or the most holy place.

At Mount Sinai, the Israelites become increasingly aware of the holiness of God. Limits are established to keep the flocks and herds from grazing on the slopes of that special mountain. Clothes are to be carefully washed. Moses alone is called up to the top of the mountain.

God seems to be teaching the people about the distance between a holy God and sinful men and women as well as the danger of presumptuously rushing into the presence of the Lord. Later, Nadab and Abihu will forget this principle, and their deaths will serve as a reminder to the rest of the Israelites (see Leviticus 10).

Leadership Lesson: While the Old Testament emphasizes the distance (transcendence) of God, the New Testament emphasizes the nearness (immanence) of God.

In Jesus Christ, God becomes flesh and comes to dwell on earth. His name is "Immanuel (which means 'God with us')" (Matthew 1:23). The writer of the book of Hebrews proposes, "Let us draw near" (Hebrews 10:22), an invitation to experience God's immanence as well as his transcendence. Now, because of what Jesus Christ has done for us, all have access to God.

In Exodus 19, with Israel camped in front of the mountain, Moses makes his way up to meet with God. He will make this trip many times. Over the next several months, his footsteps will wear a path up and down the mountain. Each time, Moses ascends to the summit and disappears into a thick cloud and consuming fire. Back and forth, up and down, representing the people to God, and then God to the people. Sinai is the place where the leader meets God. Moses goes up, and God comes down.

Leadership Lesson: Leaders benefit from a special place to regularly meet with God.

To meet regularly with God you need an identifiable, accessible place—somewhere you can go every day. That place will become special not because of the location but because of the relationship that develops there.

Israel's time at Mount Sinai is a shaping and formative experience for the nation. F. B. Meyer says, "They arrived there a fugitive and unorganized people; they left it a mighty nation in battle array, provided with a sacerdotal system that would last for centuries, as a type of the priesthood of Christ and his saints, and furnished with a code of laws and sanitary enactments that have been a model for the most civilized peoples of the world."[3]

Questions for Leadership Development

1. How would you describe the majesty of God?

2. Do you have a special place where you regularly meet with God? If not, where might you find such a place?

EIGHTEEN

THE TEN COMMANDMENTS: THE FIRST TABLET

*The fundamental basis of this nation's laws was given
to Moses on the Mount . . . If we don't have
a proper fundamental moral background,
we will finally end up with a totalitarian
government which does not believe in rights
for anybody except the State.*

Harry S. Truman[1]

While Israel is camped at the base of Mount Sinai, God summons Moses to the mountain and speaks to him of covenant. Up to this time, everything God has given the Israelites has been given freely. Now, God wants something in return: a covenant, a formal contract that calls for the Israelites to obey God's law.

God gives three different kinds of law throughout Exodus 19–40. The first kind of law (chapters 19–20) is the *moral law*, which is embodied in the Ten Commandments. The second kind of law (chapters 21–24) is the *civil law*, which includes governing laws addressing how a theocracy should function. The third kind of law (chapters 25–40) is the *ceremonial law*. This is the religious law, addressing how the tabernacle is to be constructed and how various ceremonies are to be performed. The ceremonial law is also detailed in the book of Leviticus.

These three types of law—moral, civil, and ceremonial—raise a question for us today: how much of the Old Testament law should still be observed? The accepted view is that the moral law is binding, to be observed because it flows from the character of God and is the very basis for civilization. If God's moral law is disregarded, civilization breaks down. This view also holds that the civil law is *not* binding today. It was given to a unique nation—Israel—at a time when it was a theocracy, which is a nation ruled by God. This view holds that civil governments should establish their own laws. Lastly, it is accepted that we do not need to honor the ceremonial law because it has already been fulfilled in Jesus Christ; thus, we are not obligated to keep it.

So, let's turn our attention to the moral law, which has the most relevance today. The Ten Commandments, also known as the Decalogue ("the ten words"), are the heart of God's moral law.[2] These commands represent the God-directed, God-empowered, God-reflecting behavior that distinguishes us as the people of God.

Admired for their brevity and flawless language, the Ten Commandments codify in a handful of words appropriate human behavior, generation after generation, century after century. The commandments are relevant, simple, to the point, and easy to understand.

The commandments reveal how the Israelites are to live as the redeemed people of God. "Stated in the absolutes, as the incontestable will of God,"[3] they provide "practical guidance for the common person."[4] In short, the Ten Commandments are God's instructions to his people on how to live in community. They provide God-given boundaries for life and are meant to keep us from harm.

More than a list of rules that help us hold society together, Peter Enns says they also are "the means by which the divine ordering of chaos at the cosmic level is actualized in the social sphere, whereby God's will is done on earth as it is in heaven."[5]

The First Tablet: Loving God

The Ten Commandments begin with God and our relationship to him. Everything begins with God, including any right relationship we have with other people. The first four commandments (Exodus 20:1–11) define our vertical responsibilities to God as we love him with all our heart, soul, and strength (Deuteronomy 6:5). The last six commandments (Exodus 20:12–17) define our horizontal commitments to others, which are captured in Leviticus with the command "Love your neighbor as yourself" (19:18).

#1: Holy God
"You shall have no other gods before me."

The first commandment (Exodus 20:3) requires that we believe in the existence of a single, supreme God, and it "gets at the heart of what it means to be God's people."[6] There is one God: Yahweh. God demands our exclusive worship. He is a jealous God, and his insistence on monotheism is a unique feature of Israel's religion. Enns says, "In distinction to every other people of the ancient world, they are to worship one and only God, Yahweh. In this way, Israel's uniqueness, her absolute 'holiness' and separateness vis-à-vis the surrounding nations, is broadcast loud and clear. The appeal to have one God, of course, is to Israel alone."[7]

As a preface to the Ten Commandments, God says, "I am the LORD your God, who brought you out of Egypt, out of the land of slavery" (Exodus 20:2). In doing so, he reminds us that the God who commands is also the God of grace. He has taken the initiative and acted to bring about the freedom of Israel. He has come down to free his own people, but this freedom means they must separate themselves from the worship of every other god. This points to the exclusive claim of God on the lives of his people and his demand of complete loyalty. Gerhard Von Rad suggests that "what the first commandment asks is the question of confidence—in whom do you really trust?"[8]

Leadership Lesson: **Remember, God is God and you aren't. Nor is anyone else.**

It is important to be on the alert against giving any object, any ideology, or any person the place reserved for God alone. Our allegiance is to God.

#2: Holy Worship
"You shall not make for yourself an image."

If the first commandment is about worshiping the right God, then "the second commandment is about worshiping the right God the right way."[9] We are not to worship God with images. There are to be no idols.

Idols cannot represent the Creator, since nothing created can adequately represent him. Junia Pokrifka says, "The fact that only humans are created in the image of God implies that only they can provide the legitimate images of God to other creatures, rather than creatures providing images of God to humans."[10]

The second commandment also speaks to the separation of Israel's practices from those of their neighbors: "The idol worship of the pagan nations was not only illogical and unbiblical, but it was intensely immoral (temple prostitutes and fertility rites), inhuman (sacrificing children), and demonic (1 Corinthians 10:10–22)."[11]

God prohibits Israel from making an idol in the form of any created thing. "Does 'idol' refer to an idol of one of the gods spoken of in verse 3, or does it include any sort of representation of Yahweh himself?" Peter Enns says that the command has a twofold intent: Israel is not to worship other gods, nor are they to worship Yahweh in ways that even bear resemblance to other nations.[12]

Images mislead us. They are inadequate, introduce distortions, obscure the glory of God, and distort the reality of God. James Boice says, "A representation of God is always less than God, and to that extent God is dishonored by bringing his glory down to a greatly inferior level."[13]

When God issues this second command, he includes a promise to those who obey and a warning to those who disobey. If the people disobey, consequences will last for a long time. If the people obey, blessings will last for an even longer time.

Leadership Lesson: Don't adore anything that has been created.

Don't make an idol out of your corporation, school, church, sports team, or favorite mascot or logo. The temptation is to make a god out of an image we have created and then worship it. Nothing we create is to be worshiped, and nothing God created is to be worshiped either—including other people.

#3: Holy Name

"You shall not misuse the name of the LORD your God."

The third commandment instructs us to treat God's name with utmost respect. God's name is to be honored, not misused, because the name of God represents God. To take God's name in vain is to misrepresent God's name. It is not just a prohibition against using foul language. It is a call to let our words reflect the character of the One who created us.

Leadership Lesson: Don't give in to the temptation to use the name of God to achieve your own purposes.

To use the divine name in ways that promote a personal agenda is to use God's name in vain. Leaders should avoid the temptation to use God's name to put a divine seal of approval on personal opinion. As Stephen Green says, "Ancient Israel is prohibited from making its religion into a weapon with which it could have its way with people . . . People who have a calling from God or a status in the community that places them in a position of declaring in some way the word of the Lord must take great care in the use of the divine name."[14]

#4: Holy Day
"Remember the Sabbath day by keeping it holy."

The fourth commandment is the first of only two commands stated in the positive. Remembering the Sabbath requires that we set aside one day in seven for rest. According to Exodus 20:11, God rested on the seventh day after creating heaven and earth and all that is in them. As God rested and made the seventh day holy, so humans are to rest and make the day holy. Genesis 2 reveals that human work is participation with God in the work of creation, by keeping the earth beautiful and productive. Pokrifka says, "Sabbath keeping is an act of creation keeping."[15]

The Sabbath, in the Old Testament, is not understood primarily as the day on which some special service of worship is held. Rather, it is primarily a day to cease work. Von Rad refers to the Sabbath as "a sacrifice of rest,"[16] adding, "The Sabbath is the day of rest; for rest it has been appointed and for nothing else."[17] Sabbath is a day a person does not fill with usual activity. Rather, it is a day "one gives back to God clean and unused."[18] The Sabbath is to be observed by all—rich and poor, slave and free.

Leadership Lesson: Sabbath is how humanity experiences a weekly recalibration to a healthy rhythm.

The last thing God created before resting was us, which means our first full day on earth was Sabbath. The first thing we did as creatures was to rest with God. "By resting on the seventh day, Israel is not just following God's command, but actually following God's lead."[19]

Sabbath is a day of stability, a day in which life is tuned to the rhythm of creation. It is designed to be a day of untroubled serenity. Sabbath provides a rhythm to life and establishes a seven-day week. The seventh day is holy—set apart, different. It belongs entirely to God.

Smart leaders do dumb things when they are overly fatigued and physically exhausted. Sabbath helps ensure that does not happen by maintaining a divinely inspired rhythm of working and resting.

Sabbath rest is designed not only into the rhythm of a week but also the rhythm of years. In the Old Testament, we find a command to give land rest every seven years (Exodus 23:10–11). And the fiftieth year (after the seventh sabbatical year) is the Year of Jubilee. Pokrifka says, "The years of Sabbath and Jubilee reflect the ideal state of existence in peace, rest, freedom, provision, and worship that humans enjoyed at the time of creation and will enjoy in eternity."[20] The sabbatical year law also mandates the emancipation of slaves, cancellation of debt, and fallowing of the land (see Exodus 21:2; Leviticus 25:2–5; Deuteronomy 15:9, 12).

Questions for Leadership Development

1. What authority do the Ten Commandments have today?

2. What effect does the keeping (or breaking) of the Ten Commandments have on society?

3. How does your practice of Sabbath-keeping impact your leadership?

— NINETEEN —

THE TEN COMMANDMENTS: THE SECOND TABLET

No man can break any of the Ten Commandments.
He can only break himself against them.

G. K. Chesterton

Legend has it that the first tablet Moses receives contains the first four commandments. Those commandments are particularly vertical in nature, and deal with our conduct toward God. The second tablet contains the last six commandments. Those commandments are particularly horizontal in nature, and deal with our conduct toward our neighbor. The last six commandments address what it means to live in community.

For Jesus, the entire Law can be summarized by the call to love God and love others (see Matthew 22:37–40; Mark 12:29–31; Luke 10:27). This is the essence of holy living. The last six commandments call us to deeply honor others.

#5: Honor Parents
"Honor your father and mother."

The fifth commandment addresses the most basic of human relationships: that between parents and children. This relationship is the beginning of society.

Respect for parents is a universal virtue valued by all cultures. There are two main implications of this commandment. First, children should obey their parents' instructions. Second, children have a responsibility for elderly parents. The fifth commandment tells us to hold our parents in high esteem at all times and relate to them with dignity and deference. We are to care for them in their old age.

This commandment is the first to come with a promise. God says that when we honor our parents we will "live long in the land the LORD your God is giving you" (Exodus 20:12). As each generation honors and cares for parents, the prospects for a good life for the society as a whole significantly increases. A society that honors and cares for its older members will experience blessings.

Leadership Lesson: So much of society depends on what is taught and learned in the home.

The early relationship between parent and child is where respect, obedience, and appropriate behavior are first learned. It is also where children learn to honor authority. As parents and children age, the relationship often evolves from dependence to interdependence to independence and then, finally, back to dependence. A deep respect and loving appreciation should mark all of these stages.

#6: Honor Life
"You shall not murder."

One wonders what deep emotional memory stirred within Moses when he saw the sixth commandment etched in the stone tablet. When God said, "Thou shalt not kill," was Moses reminded of that hot-blooded afternoon in Egypt when he took the life of the Egyptian?

In the sixth commandment, God commands no murder. Violence brings chaos to a society, and murder is the ultimate form of violence, which the Bible treats with great seriousness. Human life is sacred and not ours to take vengefully.

This is not a prohibition against *any* taking of human life; *murder* is differentiated from *killing*. There is legitimate and illegitimate killing in the Old Testament. Jonathan Kirsch says this commandment is "not a complete prohibition against the taking of a human life; the verb used in the Hebrew text referred specifically to a type of slaying which called forth blood vengeance."[1] The prohibition here does not include killing in war, judicial execution, or self-defense.[2] This commandment strictly forbids killing with forethought and malice.

Leadership Lesson: God calls us to honor life.

The commandment saying no to murder is at its heart a call to say yes to life. Junia Pokrifka says, "Wherever life is in danger (due to war, violence, lack of shelter and nourishment, and lack of proper medical care), this commandment summons God's people to sustain life and to reflect on all the implications and challenges of its call. . . . This commandment calls us to be givers and not takers of life."[3]

#7: Honor Marriage
"You shall not commit adultery."

The seventh commandment forbids adultery. God established the institution of marriage in the garden of Eden (Genesis 2:22–24), and the marriage relationship will be the metaphor most often used to describe the covenant relationship between God and Israel as well as between Jesus and the church.

The health of society is dependent upon the health of the families in that society. Fidelity to the marriage covenant is key to strong and healthy families. There is a biblical standard for sexual expression, which is why "God wants the physical intimacy of the marriage bond to be maintained."[4] Pokrifka says that in contrast to other societies, this commandment calls the Israelites to marital chastity and faithfulness. "The intention of the command is to prohibit all extramarital sex for married/betrothed men and married/betrothed women and all unmarried men and women."[5]

Leadership Lesson: **God's people are called to faithfulness in all relationships and, notably, in marriage.**

Faithfulness in the relationship between husband and wife should reflect faithfulness in the relationship God has with his people. Fidelity to the marriage relationship, perhaps more than any other, reveals the character of a leader.

Moses could never have anticipated how significant this commandment would become for our culture. As the concept of marriage is debated, redefined, and in some cases dismissed altogether, marriage remains a primary relationship through which the people of God can bear witness to the world. Marriage may be one of the most significant areas where spiritual leadership is needed.

#8: Honor Property
"You shall not steal."

The eighth commandment can be easily summarized: "No stealing!" This command forbids robbery, embezzlement, and dishonesty in business dealings as well (see Deuteronomy 25:13–16). The unauthorized taking of another's possession is wrong. This behavior does violence to the peace of the community.

Leadership Lesson: Taking from another what is not rightfully yours is doubly wrong.

First, stealing from your neighbor undermines God's provision for them. Second, stealing from your neighbor is doubting God's ability to provide for your needs.

Leaders who succumb to the temptation to take what does not belong to them not only ruin their own reputation but also do damage to the institutions they represent and are called to serve. This is true whether the organization is a business, an institution of higher education, the government, or a church. In addition to not stealing, leaders must also take steps to ensure the proper checks and balances are established to prevent others from stealing.

#9: Honor Truth

"You shall not give false testimony."

The ninth commandment is also easily summarized: "No lying!" Truth-telling is essential for the administration of justice. False witnesses are universally condemned in both ancient and modern cultures.

This command refers not to lying in general but specifically to bearing false testimony in court.[6] Still, the commandment has implications far beyond the courtroom. Individuals and institutions are capable of creating a narrative that serves selfish agendas rather than the truth. When the facts are distorted in any arena, justice is perverted and society suffers.

Leadership Lesson: Lying jeopardizes community.

The proclamation of truth is an affirmation of reality. Falsehood, fabrication, and deceit create a false reality. Truth-telling is paramount for the health and well-being of communities, organizations, families, and churches.

#10: Honor Contentment

"You shall not covet."

The last of the commandments is focused more on attitude than behavior. Coveting is not a crime that can be prosecuted in the same way stealing or perjury can be prosecuted. Coveting is an attitude of the heart.

To covet is to yearn after the possessions of others. It is to be dissatisfied and ungrateful for what God has provided you, and instead desire what God has provided your neighbor—often leading you to attempt to secure that thing.

What is the opposite of coveting? Contentment. Stephen Green says, "Coveting is ultimately a life lived without gratitude for the opportune gifts that are received by oneself and one's neighbor. It lacks the basic belief in the story of God's providence and benevolence."[7] I also like how Pokrifka explains it. She says that coveting is the opposite of *covenanting*. "Coveting ends in unlawful acquisitions whereas covenanting leads to the caring and loving treatment of the neighbor and his or her property."[8]

Leadership Lesson: A leader's attitude will eventually result in actions.

That is why it is important for you to guard your heart. Self-awareness, a mindfulness of the attitudes in your heart, can help you address destructive feelings before they bear the fruit of disastrous actions.

The Ten Commandments are expectations for how God's people are to behave. These laws are grounded in the character of a holy God. The pagan nations might lie, but the people of God are honest because God is truth. The pagan nations may steal, but God's people honor the possessions of others because we view possessions as gifts from God's hand. The pagan nations may practice infidelity to their spouses, but God's people practice covenant faithfulness because God is faithful.

God spends forty days and forty nights revealing the Law to Moses on Mount Sinai. When he finishes, he gives Moses a pair of stone tablets on which are written the commands, each one "inscribed by the finger of God" (Exodus 31:18). Moses takes the two new tablets and heads down the mountain to share them with the people. But before Moses reaches the foot of the mountain, the Ten Commandments will be broken, in more ways than one.

Questions for Leadership Development

1. Why does God spend more than half of the Ten Commandments instructing us on our relationships with others?

2. Why is marital faithfulness of such importance to God? What are deeper levels of faithfulness you can exhibit in this area?

3. What do the Ten Commandments reflect about the nature and character of God?

— TWENTY —

THE GOLDEN CALF: UNHOLY WORSHIP

The story of the golden calf is about the human tendency to believe that human-made items can resolve our fear, anxiety, sense of lostness, despair, and hopelessness.

C. Andrew Doyle[1]

One wonders what Moses is thinking as he makes his way down the mountain, cradling the two tablets of the Law in his arms. He had climbed the mountain accompanied by Aaron, Aaron's two sons, and the seventy elders of Israel. There on the mountain they worshiped and experienced God's presence in an extraordinary manner (Exodus 24:9–11). Then Moses was summoned to climb farther up the mountain with his aide, Joshua, to meet with God.

While Moses is experiencing the splendor of God's presence on the mountain, God makes a distressing announcement: "Go down, because your people, whom you brought up out of Egypt, have become corrupt" (32:7). Much like what happens centuries later after the transfiguration of Jesus (Luke 9:28–43), Moses will go from the majesty on the mountain to the mess in the valley.

As Moses traces his way back down the mountain, he hears a strange sound coming from the camp. Joshua, the military leader, mistakes the noise for the sound of war. The commotion, however, proves to be something even more disturbing. It is the sound of obscene revelry. Despairing of Moses's return, the people have demanded that Aaron fashion them gods to lead them. They have grown impatient, saying, "As for this fellow Moses who brought us up out of Egypt, we don't know what has happened to him" (Exodus 32:1). Aaron, apparently more eager to please the people than to please God, gives in to their demand.

Leadership Lesson: The maturity of a group can be evaluated, in part, by how long they can tolerate the absence of the leader before chaos sets in.

For the Israelites, forty days is their limit. After forty days, the group becomes dysfunctional. Some followers demand the presence of a leader before they will behave. Israel does not know how to live by faith and trust God without a leader present.

"Wait on the Lord" is valuable advice to both leaders and followers. A lack of patience can lead to spiritual disobedience. Seeking quick resolutions often leads to unfortunate consequences. The patience to wait for the right time to act is as valuable a leadership asset as the ability to recognize what the right time is. Of course, it is never the right time to do the wrong thing.

Moses is on the mountain for a long time—forty days. While Moses is on the mountain, the Israelites decide that creating an image of God is more preferred than God himself. When they ask Aaron to make a god, Aaron accommodates them. Remarkably, the people respond willingly, even eagerly, to Aaron's request that they surrender their gold. Out of their gold, Aaron fashions a calf that the Israelites proclaim to be the god that brought them out of Egypt. They begin to worship the idol, breaking from all restraint to participate in an unholy riot. Chaos becomes evident in the ranks of the Israelites. Apparently, the worship of the calf is accompanied with the licentious orgies that are a recognized part of Egyptian idolatry.

Leadership Lesson: What or whom you worship will determine *how* you worship.

The golden calf is an image that is reminiscent of Egyptian pagan worship. Thus, pagan behavior accompanies the Israelites' wrongful worship. It should not be surprising that the character, traits, and values of the object of our worship will also affect the way we worship.

When Moses comes near enough to see the calf and the dancing, the anger that characterizes his earlier life breaks out again. He reacts to what he sees taking place in the camp by smashing the sacred tablets in fury, shattering them on the mountain (v. 19). His act is possibly symbolic: the people are breaking the law of God, so Moses breaks the tablets of the Law as a visual demonstration. He then declares, "You have committed a great sin" (v. 30). We find a similar reaction when Jesus enters the temple and sees that the place of prayer has become a center of commerce. Moses throws tablets. Jesus throws tables. Their anger is justified. Their indignation is righteous.

Leadership Lesson: **Unless dealt with, the same sin can hang on for generations.**

This is not the only golden calf Israel will worship. This apostasy of Israel will be repeated during the time of King Jeroboam, the first king of the northern kingdom, after civil war splits the ten northern tribes off from Judah and Benjamin. First Kings 12 contains the account of how Jeroboam sets up a golden calf at both Bethel and Dan. Because the temple is located in the south, Jeroboam is afraid that those in the northern kingdom will be loyal to the southern kingdom. So he sets up two worship centers as rivals to Jerusalem, with golden calves as the objects of worship (vv. 25–33). The similarities are striking: "Jeroboam was such a dedicated sinner that he reveled in reenacting the very worst sin in the collective memory of ancient Israel—the 'sin par excellence'—and doing so no less than twenty-one times."[2]

As was the case with Israel, the generational influence of some sin is seen today. Idolatry can be passed along from parent to child, as can prejudice, greed, substance abuse, and an assortment of other sins. Jesus alone has the power to break generational curses.

Moses destroys the idol, grinds it to powder, burns it, mixes the ashes with water, and pours it down the throats of the faithless men and women who have been dancing around the idols only moments before. Moses also rebukes Aaron publicly. Aaron responds with a lame, self-serving, and blame-passing excuse. First, he blames the people. "It was *their* idea," he says. Next, he blames Moses for staying on the mountain too long. Finally, he affixes the responsibility to fate, claiming to have thrown gold into a fire only to see the calf emerge on its own.

Leadership Lesson: Some leaders give people what they want, instead of what they need.

Moses comes down the mountain prepared to give the people what they need. He then discovers that in his absence Aaron has given them what they want. Maybe that's one of the reasons God chose Moses and not Aaron. God's people can't afford leaders who don't know the difference between needs and wants.[3]

The people are out of control, and Aaron is responsible for allowing it. To restore order, drastic measures will be taken. Moses asks, "Who is on the Lord's side?" and the Levites respond by rallying to Moses's side, ready to fulfill his directions. At Moses's request, the Levites pick up their swords, and a purge of the Israelites begins. The sin of idolatry will be treated with severity as three thousand people are slain. The Levites accomplish their grim duty, no doubt targeting the ringleaders of the orgy. The anarchy ends.

The next day, when the camp is filled with mourning over the newly made graves and the awful realization has set in on the people, Moses's indignation gives way to bitter sorrow and pity. Back up the mountain he trudges, this time to intercede on behalf of his people.

God is angry enough to kill Aaron, but Moses intercedes for his brother (see Deuteronomy 9:20). Because of Israel's sin, God determines not to accompany them any farther on their journey toward the promised land. Because the Israelites are stiff-necked and God might be tempted to destroy them on the way, he determines to send an angel with them instead of going himself (Exodus 33:2–3).

But Moses reminds God that rejecting Israel at this point will cause widespread implications, including a loss of the exodus's meaning, giving Israel's enemies a reason to rejoice.

Next, Moses asks God if he has forgotten his covenant with Abraham. When Moses names the patriarchs, he says, "Abraham, Isaac, and *Israel*" (32:13)—not Jacob, which is what is usually said. Moses uses Jacob's new name Israel because that is the covenant name of the people for whom Moses is pleading. Moses is reminding God of the several promises made to the patriarchs and that God is about to destroy those with whom God made a covenant.

Lastly, God says, "I'll destroy them and save you." But Moses counters by saying, "Save them and destroy me," offering to make himself a substitute (v. 32). This is powerful intercession. Moses intervenes for the Israelites, becoming their advocate. In response to Moses's intercession, God turns from his anger.

Peter Enns says, "If we wish to point to the episode that makes Moses truly special, that makes him deserving of all the honor, attention, and respect he has received through the ages, it is his shielding an ungrateful people from the end they most certainly deserve, even if it means taking their place and bearing the full weight, horror, and ignominy of God's anger. The world will not see the likes of this again for many generations."[4] Moses's intervention is seen by some as christological. "Moses's unprecedented act of intercession, offering up his own life for the sake of the Israelites, prefigures the ultimate intercession Christ makes for sinful humanity by utterly giving himself up as an atoning sacrifice."[5]

Leadership Lesson: **Good leaders intercede for their people.**

Responsible leaders will put the needs of the people they serve above their own needs. Moses provides an inspiring example of this kind of leadership. He is a good shepherd who makes the needs of the sheep a priority. When Moses refuses God's offer to make him the only survivor and start a new nation, he shows us that leadership is about responsibility, not privilege. Leaders intercede for their people when they are at risk.

Moses is instructed to carve two fresh tablets from stone so God may inscribe them. Moses, tablets in hand, once again ascends the mountain, where he stays another forty days and forty nights. Moses and his people will benefit from the God who gives second chances.

Questions for Leadership Development

1. In what ways is the generational influence of sin evident today?

2. As a leader, how do you intercede for those you serve?

3. What might be identified as sacred cows (or golden calves) in your worshiping community?

— TWENTY-ONE —

THE CLEFT OF THE ROCK: SHOW ME YOUR GLORY, LORD

Rock of ages, cleft for me,
let me hide myself in thee.
Augustus Toplady[1]

Everybody needs a place to regularly meet with God, and Moses has such a place—the tent of meeting. Whenever Moses enters the tent of meeting, which is located outside the camp, the pillar of cloud comes down in front of the tent door, and God speaks to him there "as one speaks to a friend" (Exodus 33:7–11). Joshua also frequents the tent of meeting with Moses, usually staying there even after Moses leaves.

In Exodus 33, Moses enters the tent of meeting and makes three requests of God. His first request is to have greater knowledge of God. Moses wants to know God, his ways, and his favor. Seeking this more intimate awareness, Moses asks, "If you are pleased with me, teach me your ways so I may know you and continue to find favor with you" (v. 13).

Leadership Lesson: Those who lead the people of God must desire to intimately know God and his ways.

Moses already knows God, but he wants to know him with even more familiarity. Leaders grow in their understanding of God and his ways by regularly spending time with God in prayer and engaging with God though his Word.

Moses's second request is that the presence of God accompany the Israelites on their journey. God has said he will send his angel with the Israelites but not go himself. Moses requests that God himself accompany his people, declaring, "If your Presence does not go with us, do not send us up from here" (v. 15). It is as though Moses is saying, "I'd rather stay right here in the desert for the rest of my life than go to Canaan without you." The Lord agrees to grant Moses's request, promising not only his presence but also his rest. The promise of God's presence is a gift that brings confident assurance.

Leadership Lesson: There is a significant connection between the presence of God and the ability of a leader to rest in confident assurance.

The presence of God is essential, and so is the rest that God's presence provides. Moses is unwilling to experience the milk and honey of Canaan if it means God's blessing without God's presence. He recognizes that the greatest blessing of life is not the gifts God may provide; the greatest blessing of life is the sense of God's presence.

Additionally, when God promises Moses his presence, he also promises his rest. The significance of rest for leaders cannot be overstated. The importance of rest is as applicable today as it was in Moses's time.

———————

Moses's third request is to experience the glory of God. Moses asks, "Now show me your glory" (v. 18). God's glory is the manifestation of his magnificent presence. Moses wants to experience the intense, visible demonstration of the presence of God.

God responds by announcing that he will cause his glory to pass by Moses. Moses will indeed see God's glory but only the back of God, not his face. God places Moses in the cleft of a rock and shields him with his hand as his glory passes by. If God removes his hand, Moses will surely die. Without this divine protection, Moses could not survive the experience.

———————

Leadership Lesson: God gives as much of himself as we desire and can bear.

There seem to be two kinds of people in the world—those who long to see God and be seen by him and those who, like Adam and Eve hiding in the garden, do not. God reveals as much of himself to Moses as Moses desires and can endure.

———————

Once again, Moses trudges up the mountain. No doubt this time his sense of anticipation is greatly heightened. He is instructed to chisel out two new tablets of stone. For forty days, Moses will neither eat nor drink as the Law is given and the Ten Commandments are once again etched on stone tablets.

Leadership Lesson: Drawing near to God takes effort.

For Moses, drawing near means laboring up the mountain time and time again. For us, drawing near requires intentionally creating space in our crowded lives and deliberately pausing our hectic routines.

Moses's most intimate experience with God occurs in the cleft of a rock on Sinai. We imagine the narrow place in the rock allowed only ray of light to enter. Yet "this ray—piercing dense is absorbed into Moses's face and leaves him mysteriously radiant."[2] Here, Moses discovers that he has never felt more protected or more vulnerable than in the presence of God.

The intimacy Moses enjoys with God is unique in the Old Testament and will have a profound and lasting effect. When Moses comes down the mountain, he is a changed man—even in his outward appearance. He has been exposed to the splendor of God, and something of that brightness remains on his face. Moses returns from the experience of being in God's presence with an afterglow.

The glow is so bright the Israelites cannot look at him. Because they are frightened, Moses puts on a veil to cover his shining face, thus preventing the people from looking upon the full radiance (34:29–35). That veil becomes a symbol of Moses's authority and intimacy with God.

Leadership Lesson: Time spent in the presence of God transforms a leader in ways that others recognize.

As Craig Barnes says, "Five minutes into the sermon on Sundays, everyone can tell if God and I are getting along okay."[3] Being with God is an experience that changes leaders. When Moses is with God,

the results are obvious to Aaron and all of Israel. The rays at first in-
timidate and then attract. Spending time with God is a transformative
experience that prepares leaders for more effective service.

In 2 Corinthians 3:7–18, Paul suggests that, although Moses's
veil was originally used to protect the people from his shining
face, eventually it protects Moses as well. Paul says the reason
Moses continues to wear the veil is so the Israelites will not see
that the glory is fading away. At first, the veil conceals the glory.
Then, the veil conceals the fading of the glory. In time, the veil
becomes a facade, a mask.

Leadership Lesson: Leaders need to be appropriately transparent.

It is one thing for Moses to protect the people from the glow. It
is another thing for Moses to keep the people from becoming aware
of the fading of that glow. Veils become masks when they are used
to hide a leader's life. Transparency should be valued above facades.

Questions for Leadership Development

1. Where is your tent of meeting?

2. In what ways do you cultivate a greater understanding of God?

3. When was the last time you stepped away from your routine to spend time alone with God? What are ways you can step away in the future?

4. How transparent should a leader be?

TWENTY-TWO

BEZALEL AND OHOLIAB: THE TABERNACLE

*Then have them make a sanctuary for me,
and I will dwell among them.*

Exodus 25:8

During Moses's stay on Mount Sinai, he receives instructions for building the tabernacle—a portable structure intended to be a visible symbol of God's presence. The tabernacle will be the primary symbol of God's continued presence with his people until King Solomon builds the temple on Mount Moriah in Jerusalem. Erected at the center of the Israelite camp, with the tents of the people of Israel on all four sides, the tabernacle is not only the largest structure in the camp but also the most beautiful.

Peter Enns, eager to link the exodus narratives to the creation story, says that thinking "of the tabernacle as an act of cosmic re-creation is precisely what the building of the tabernacle originally intended to convey." The splendor of the materials used— fine fabrics, precious metals, and stones—reflect the goodness of the created world. "The precise and perfect dimensions of the tabernacle indicate a sense of order amid chaos."[1]

On the Sabbath, the tabernacle will become the place where holy space and holy time intersect. It is both a physical representation of God's presence and a visible reminder of God's holiness. The tabernacle will be a place to worship, a place to connect with God, and, according to Warren Wiersbe, a reminder of the Israelites' responsibility: "Having the Lord dwelling in the camp was a great privilege for the nation of Israel (Rom. 9:4-5), for no other nation had the living God in their midst. But the privilege brought with it a great responsibility, for it meant that the camp of Israel had to be a holy place where a holy God could dwell."[2]

Leadership Lesson: God's people need holy time *and* holy space.

As the Sabbath is holy time, the tabernacle is holy space. "Weekly Sabbath worship is on holy ground in holy time," says Enns. "There is no more holy spot on the face of the earth than the tabernacle on the Sabbath."[3] Everything about the tabernacle and the manifest glory points to the holiness of God. The tabernacle teaches two concepts: First, it teaches that God is immanent—mercifully condescending to be with his people and dwell among them. Second, it teaches that God is transcendent—his ways are far above our ways. Enns says the tabernacle is "a piece of holy ground amid a world that has lost its way."[4]

The Israelites are commanded to build the tabernacle as a place for God's glory to dwell, and the tribe of Levi is set apart as servants to minister to him in that place. The tabernacle—what it looks like, how it functions, what it represents—is a continual reminder of who God is.

Wiersbe describes the moveable nature of the tabernacle:

The tabernacle was a portable tent; it was not a place of assembly like a modern-day church building. Each time Israel broke camp, the Levites dismantled the tent carefully, wrapped the furnishings in their coverings, and carried them until the Lord told the people to stop. (The curtains and the framework were carried on wagons.) At the new location, the tabernacle was reassembled and the furniture put into place (Numbers 3–4). Each piece of furniture had rings attached through which poles were fitted so they could be carried in the wilderness march. The poles on the ark were never to be removed (Exodus 25:15–1 Kings 8:8).[5]

Exodus 31 tells us how God provides not only all the instructions for the building of the tabernacle but also the workmen. Two of the workmen are specifically mentioned by name. God assigns Bezalel and Oholiab the task of overseeing the building of the tabernacle and furnishings (31:1–11; 35:30–36:7). Bezalel, from the tribe of Judah, will be in charge of the construction project. Oholiab, from the tribe of Dan, will be his chief assistant. Part of their job is to direct an assembly of artisans—"skilled workers and designers" (35:35).

While several master artists will complete the construction of the tabernacle, Bezalel is given sole responsibility for making the ark of the covenant. His skills include carpentry, jewelry making, and metalwork (31:2–5). Oholiab specializes in the areas of engraving, weaving, and designing tapestry (38:23).

Leadership Lesson: **Artistic talent is from God and can be used in his service and for his glory.**

Leaders need those gifted in artistic expression to express vision in ways that inspire and point people to God's holiness. For Moses, the artists are weavers and metalworkers. For modern-day leaders, the needed artists may be architects, graphic designers, musicians, or the like. Junia Pokrifka says, "The ultimate purpose of human creativity

and ingenuity is to capture and execute God's vision for divine plea-
sure, which, in turn, serves humanity. This understanding of art stands
against art as a means of self-expression or a quest."[6] When places
of worship reflect great beauty, majestic art, and inspiring design, it
becomes easy for worshipers to appreciate the greatness of God.

The Lord (not Moses) chooses Bezalel, who is filled with "the
Spirit of God, with wisdom, with understanding, with knowledge and with all kinds of skills" (31:3). God has given Bezalel
the ability to create something useful *and* beautiful. Pokrifka says,
"Already a master in his field of artistry, Yahweh fills Bezalel with
the Spirit of God (see Exodus 31:3). What is communicated to
Moses in visions and words, Bezalel is able to implement in artistic construction. He is also able to teach and to direct others
so that more artisans learn to execute the work (Exodus 35:34)."[7]

Leadership Lesson: Even the work of a master artist is taken to
another level when that artist is filled with the Spirit of God.

Bezalel and Oholiab are already recognized master artists in their
fields, but when they are filled with the Spirit of God, greater creativity, ingenuity, invention, and inspiration result. Pokrifka says, "What
Jesus says to Nicodemus aptly applies to art and creative endeavors:
'Flesh gives birth to flesh, but the Spirit gives birth to spirit' (John
3:6). While creativity is part of the divine image, unsanctified creativity falls short of divine glory since the divine image in which we are
created has been corrupted by sin. However, sanctified, consecrated,
and anointed creativity, as part of the restored divine image in and
through Christ, glorifies God."[8] Sanctified imagination allows artists to
produce work that reflects the glory of the divine.

Bezalel and Oholiab are singled out for the task of putting all the information together and building the tabernacle and all its furnishings. They are equipped and enabled to do the job. They have the skill and wisdom needed, and Moses makes sure they have the resources (both human and material) to construct the tabernacle and its furniture. While general instructions are given for the kind and design of the furnishings, there is still room for creativity to be expressed.

Leadership Lesson: **When delegating responsibility to capable individuals, leave room for creative expression.**

Pokrifka says,

In the instructions for the tabernacle and its furnishings, only main descriptions are given: the material to be used, the dimensions, the main structure, and the general placement of objects. Details are left "to the divinely anointed artisan's brilliant creativity." The text balances a concern for obedient adherence to the divine instructions with a respect for an artistic freedom concerning many of the details. Where no detailed descriptions are given, one expects that artists' unique contributions were encouraged.[9]

The tabernacle is a portable house of worship, the precursor to the temple, located at the center of the camp, encircled by the tents of the people. The writer of Exodus spends more time on instructions for building the tabernacle and its furnishings than on the story of the plagues and the actual exodus, indicating the tabernacle's significance.

The materials for the construction of the tabernacle—precious metals, expensive yarns and linen, precious stones, and gems—are originally provided by the Egyptians. Wiersbe describes the materials, saying, "Several different kinds of material were needed:

precious metal (gold, silver), bronze, fabrics (yarn, fine linen, and goat's hair), wood, skins, olive oil, spices, and precious stones. It's been estimated that a ton of gold was used in the tabernacle as well as over three tons of silver. Where did all this wealth come from? For one thing, the Jews had 'spoiled' the Egyptians before leaving the land (Exodus 12:35–36), and no doubt there were also spoils from the victory over Amalek (17:8–16). God saw to it that they had everything they needed to build the tabernacle just as he had designed it."[10]

Leadership Lesson: It is a wonderful thing when the people of God are inclined to give generously.

The people brought so much, gave so much, that Moses finally had to tell them to stop giving (36:6–7). F. B. Meyer says that God's plan for the tabernacle and its furnishings is commensurate with the people's resources. God has already provided the resources needed to construct the tabernacle and its furnishings. All that is necessary is the willingness of the people and the talent of the artisans. The materials are already in the possession of the people. Meyer continues, "God never gives . . . a pattern without making himself responsible for the provision of all materials needed for its execution. If the materials are not forthcoming, you may seriously question whether you are not working on a plan of your own."[11]

Questions for Leadership Development

1. What spaces in your life have been holy spaces?

2. What is the role of art, artists, and artistic imagination in the church?

3. In what kind of setting is it easiest for you to worship God?

TWENTY-THREE

THE TWELVE SPIES: THE MAJORITY ISN'T ALWAYS RIGHT

Ten looked at God through the difficulties.
Two looked at the difficulties through God.

F. B. Meyer[1]

The story of the twelve spies is found in Numbers 13–14, and is referenced many other times in the Bible, including Numbers 32:8–13, Deuteronomy 1:19–46, Psalm 95:10–11, and 1 Corinthians 10:5.

When the Israelites arrive at Kadesh Barnea, they find themselves within striking distance of the promised land. They decide to spy out the land by sending in a reconnaissance team before the entire group enters Canaan.

When Moses tells the story in Numbers 13, he says God tells him to send twelve spies into the promised land. Their job is to answer these questions: Are the people many or few? Are they strong or weak? Is the land good or bad? Are the towns walled or unfortified? Is the soil rich or poor? Are there trees? Is there fruit? The mission is simply to find the best route into the land and the cities located within the land. Moses knows they do not need to send spies, and when he tells the story again in Deuteronomy 1, he writes that the people insisted spies be sent.

The first mistake the people make is desiring to spy out the land. While God allows for the spies to be sent, and dictates how they will be sent, the proposal does not originate with God. The proposal originates with the Hebrews themselves (Deuteronomy 1:22). God gives the Israelites what they want, and they come to regret it. God tells Moses to pick twelve spies representing each of the twelve tribes and to send them into the land to scout it out carefully. It deserves noting that the spies are supposed to bring back a report, not a recommendation.

It takes about forty days for the spies to investigate thoroughly. As they make their way back, they travel through a valley filled with enormous grapes. They take a cluster of grapes so large that one man cannot carry it alone. The fruit has to be draped over a pole for two men to carry. Others bring bundles of figs and pomegranates that would have won first prize at any state fair. To people who have spent the last year eating manna in the wilderness, the delicacies must look sweet and irresistible.

Leadership Lesson: **Gathering firsthand information is important only if that information leads you to do the right thing.**

Some leaders seek information to help them make a good decision. Others look for data to support a decision they have already made.

The report of the spies is found in Numbers 13:26–33. Initially, none of the twelve spies disagree about what they saw. All are in agreement that the land is fruitful and desirable.

Although they come back with evidence that the land truly "does flow with milk and honey" (v. 27), most of the spies give a negative report of their findings. They are quick to point out that the land also flows with numerous enemies and fortified cities. Ten of the spies report that the Israelites will never be able to drive the Canaanites out of their walled cities, nor can they ever defeat the giants they will encounter. According to James Boice, "Ten looked at the giants, compared themselves to the giants, and felt like grasshoppers."[2] Two fix their eyes on God, and from that perspective the giants look small.

Leadership Lesson: **Focusing on problems can make the problems look greater than they really are.**

Focusing on God brings problems into true perspective, allows faith to increase, and often results in the emergence of solutions. Problems are often greater than we are, but they are never greater than God.

The two spies who give a favorable report are Caleb and Joshua. Caleb's recommendation counters the negative reports: "We should go up and take possession of the land, for we can certainly do it" (v. 30). Caleb is the representative of the tribe of Judah. He is forty years old when he goes into the promised land, and it will be thirty-eight years before he sees Canaan again. In addition, it takes seven more years to conquer the land. That means Caleb is eighty-five years old at the end of the campaign. Caleb was faithful to the end (see Joshua 14:6–14). Perhaps he understood that taking possession of the land was more like receiving an inheritance than winning a contest.[3]

Leadership Lesson: There is a difference between taking something and inheriting something.

Caleb recognizes the difference. Taking the land means relying on your own strength and effort. Inheriting the land is to receive the land as a gift. Taking the land means depending on your own ability. Inheriting the land means depending on God's gracious provision. The Israelites do not understand that the land is intended to be God's gift and that possessing the land is not dependent on their own ability.

The second mistake the Israelites make is adopting the discouraging report of the ten spies. The terrifying report is more than they can handle. Up to this point, God has showed his power countless times, yet the people find it difficult to trust and obey.

Leadership Lesson: The will of the majority is not always the will of God.

However, a majority of faithful men and women led by God's voice *can* reflect God's will and way. Challenge your people to avoid the temptation of doing what seems easiest rather than what is best.

The third mistake the Israelites make is their murmuring. "We should choose a leader and go back to Egypt," they say, forming a sort of "back to Egypt" committee (Numbers 14:4). In the midst of this rebellion, only four remain faithful to God: Moses, Aaron, Joshua, and Caleb.

As a result of the bad report, fear dominates the community. The decision is made not to enter the land. The consequence of this lack of faith and disobedience is that no man or woman presently of adult age will enter the land of promise, save Joshua and

Caleb (Deuteronomy 1:35). Even Moses himself will be excluded from entry (v. 37). However, there is a promise of hope: "And the little ones that you said would be taken captive, your children who do not yet know good from bad—they will enter the land. I will give it to them and they will take possession of it" (v. 39).

Moses "falls facedown" numerous times in the book of Numbers (14:5; 16:4, 22, 45; 20:6). On most of these occasions, his face in the sand, Moses dramatically demonstrates what it is to be at a loss for words. In Numbers 14:5, the report of the spies will lead to the crisis of a national death wish. The people are ready to stone Moses, Aaron, and Joshua before returning to Egypt.

With the people in open rebellion, God is willing to give them exactly what they are asking for. He is willing to strike them down with a plague so they will never have to face the inhabitants of the promised land. God proclaims to Moses that he will destroy the people due to their disobedience and start all over with Moses alone. Yet Moses does what he has done before. Once again, he pleads with God to pardon the people according to the greatness of his mercy. God forgives the Israelites, but the consequences for the people's rebellion are harsh. Not one of the adults living at that time except Caleb and Joshua will get to see the promised land (Numbers 14:20–25). The people's sin is forgiven, but they suffer the consequences of their rebellion.

Leadership Lesson: **It's more difficult to lead when the people who start the journey with you don't end it with you.**

Only two of the people who start the journey with Moses will finish it with him: Joshua and Caleb. A complete turnover in followers, parishioners, or work colleagues can be painful and difficult for a leader to navigate.[9]

Once again, God spares his people, although a generation will perish before Israel steps foot into the promised land. Apart from Joshua and Caleb, none of the adults who experienced the exodus will cross the Jordan. Their original cries—"If only we had died in Egypt! Or in this wilderness!" (Numbers 14:2)—come true. They will wander in the desert for thirty-eight more years, until everyone over the age of twenty who grumbles against the Lord dies (v. 29).

Leadership Lesson: God is looking for a willing generation.

In the case of the Israelites, when the faith and obedience of the present generation is lacking, God turns to the next generation to fulfill his purposes. May what was said of David be said of us, that we serve the purpose of God in our "own generation" (Acts 13:36).

Questions for Leadership Development

1. Do you tend to focus more on problems or solutions, and what bearing does that have on your leadership effectiveness?

2. How does a leader best lead when convinced that the decision of the majority is wrong?

3. Do the people you serve tend to look back or lean forward? How does effective leadership respond to the tendency?

— TWENTY-FOUR —

THE WILDERNESS: FAITH'S PROVING GROUND

. . . that vast and dreadful wilderness . . .
Deuteronomy 1:19

God's people are no strangers to the wilderness. The Old Testament book Numbers actually has several different Hebrew titles, including one translated "in the wilderness."

Rather than experiencing the richness of a land of milk and honey, the wilderness of the vast Sinai Peninsula becomes the home of the Israelites for the next four decades. None of those twenty years old or older will enter the promised land. What could have been a brief journey becomes a long sojourn as a whole generation passes away in the wilderness.

Leadership Lesson: Life works best when lived in obedience to God.

When we rebel against God, life becomes harder, and experiencing the blessings God wishes to provide us takes longer. Life is usually easier when we simply obey. It certainly would have been easier for the Israelites had they obeyed.

Still outside the promised land, Moses will now enter the third major stage of his life. The first stage of Moses's life was in a palace in Egypt. The second stage of Moses's life was in the wilderness of Midian. The third and final stage of Moses's life will take place in the wilderness of Sinai.

Leadership Lesson: **God doesn't usually tell us everything at once.**

He certainly did not tell Moses everything at once. Instead, God graciously veiled from Moses the weary journey of forty years. Some things might crush us if we knew them in their entirety. However, God does promise us grace sufficient for each day.

It is disappointing for Moses and the Israelites to know they will not enter the promised land. However, the pillar of cloud and pillar of fire continue to provide comfort. What a marvelous sight it must have been to see the cloud rise and begin to move. The priests trumpet the signal that it is time to resume the journey. Numbers 10:11–28 lists the order in which the tribes of Israel march. God has given Moses specific instructions for this as well as how they are to set up camp. The Levites are to march first, carrying the ark of the covenant. Then comes Judah, the largest tribe of all, followed by Issachar and Zebulun and the wagons bearing the tabernacle (see Numbers 7:1–9). After that comes Reuben, followed by Simeon and Gad; then the long lines of Kohathites, carrying on their shoulders the sacred furniture of the tabernacle. Then march the remaining six tribes in two great divisions. The first division is led by Ephraim, followed by Manasseh and Benjamin. The second division is led by Dan, followed by Asher and Naphtali. When they stop, the encampment is formed into a square with the tabernacle in the center and three tribes encamped on each side.

Leadership Lesson: Whom you journey beside is important.

The organization of the twelve tribes is intentional. It matters who travels together and who works together. The tribes are arranged (1) in relation to the tabernacle, and (2) in relation to one another.[1] In this way, they are assured of connection with God and with each other. As they travel, peace, harmony, and unity will be promoted among them.

So what does the desert provide the Israelites in their waiting? For starters, the wilderness will become a school of advanced leadership—a training ground for a generation who will conquer and inhabit the promised land. The desert provides them an opportunity to prepare. Before a new generation will be ready, there are lessons to be learned. In the wilderness, God's people will learn utter dependence on God, and they will discover God can be trusted.

Leadership Lesson: The question is not whether you will ever find yourself in the wilderness—you will—but what is God's purpose in your wilderness experience?

Some of the most important figures in the Bible have wilderness experiences or difficult seasons that serve to train them. David spends time in the wilderness undergoing training when King Saul seeks to kill him (see 1 Samuel 19–23). However, out of those caves emerge some of the most beautiful songs in the Bible. David needs to be broken before he can be a man after God's own heart. That happens in the wilderness.

Elijah also flees to the wilderness when Jezebel tries to kill him, but God sustains him there (see 1 Kings 19). Jesus spends a season in the wilderness of temptation, a precursor to his public ministry (see Matthew 4:1–11; Mark 1:12–13; Luke 4:1–13). Paul experiences a season of wilderness immediately after his conversion, going to Arabia for three years (see Galatians 1:11–18). We don't know much about that time, except that it was a season of preparation that led to a life of significant ministry.

People find themselves in the wilderness for many reasons: a new marriage or the loss of a marriage; a new job or the loss of a job; the birth of a child or the loss of a child. Wilderness is any place between the known that used to be and the unknown that is to come. The cause of wilderness can be varied, but the purpose is usually singular: to learn trust in and dependence on God.

God often uses the wilderness to prepare us, shaping our hearts, mind, and character for his good purposes. In the wilderness we learn lessons in humility, perseverance, self-discipline, faith, character, and how to listen to the voice of God. The familiar, comfortable, and convenient are all stripped away in the wilderness. In the wilderness we learn about ourselves and about God. We learn what is important and what is peripheral. We learn how to listen for the voice of God. The wilderness offers preparation for a fresh start.

The Israelites are guided into the wilderness by God, led by Moses, as a matter of obedience. They *stay* in the wilderness longer than necessary because of their disobedience. The wilderness may be hostile territory, but it is also intended to be temporary.

Leadership Lesson: In the wilderness "one enters the school of self-discovery"[2] as God prepares us for significant service.

The wilderness is a time for both God awareness and self-awareness. Charles Swindoll posits that God leads us "through desert places . . . so that he might humble us, that he might test us, and that the true condition of our heart might be revealed."[3] The best way to navigate the wilderness is to trust God to provide for your needs, guide you on the journey, and bring you to the other side.

The good news is this: God doesn't leave his people in the wilderness! Trust him. There will be rest for the Israelites. They will arrive at the promised land. So will you.

Questions for Leadership Development

1. Have you ever been in a wilderness season? If so, how would you describe that experience? What was God's purpose for you during that time?

2. Why is it difficult at times to trust God in the wilderness?

3. Why is it easier for God to shape and form people in the wilderness?

TWENTY-FIVE

KORAH AND THE RABBLE: DEALING WITH STIFF-NECKED PEOPLE

Do everything without grumbling or arguing.
Philippians 2:14

For forty years, Moses will deal with stiff-necked and rebellious people, some of whom pose a significant threat to his leadership. Primary among the troublemakers is Korah, who in Numbers 16 leads a large-scale revolt against Moses. Korah, joined by two hundred fifty other prominent men, directs a formidable conspiracy, significant in part because of the position Korah holds and the authority he wields.

When the people listen to the unbelieving spies, they are ready to stone Moses and Aaron and elect another leader who will take them back to Egypt. In Numbers 16 and 17, that spirit of rebellion emerges again in Korah and other leaders. The target of their rebellion is Aaron, the high priest. Korah, himself a Levite, wants to get rid of Aaron and be priest in his place.

Korah's complaint is that all the Israelites should be set apart as holy, not just Moses and Aaron. The high priesthood, he believes, should not be limited to Aaron. The unique calling, character, and office of Moses and Aaron is being contested. Korah and his followers lay claim to equal rights with Moses and Aaron, including equal access to God. This is a struggle for power. Political rebellion and mutiny are on the wind.

Leadership Lesson: **Do not be surprised if you face moments of severe opposition.**

Every true leader will encounter opposition at some point. Such is the nature of leadership. How you respond to opposition becomes the critical question. Moses provides a great model for us. He prays, acts humbly, and continues to lead. God always chooses to work through humans to lead his people. Inevitably, not everyone will accept the leaders through whom God chooses to work. Don't become fretful about those who yell, complain, cajole, or object. Rather, do what the Lord has called you to do. What matters is being faithful to the responsibility entrusted to you.

When Korah expresses his complaint to Moses, Moses immediately falls facedown before the Lord. This posture is his preferred manner of responding to discontent. Moses does not seek to vindicate himself. He does not speak on his own behalf. He leaves his vindication to God (see Numbers 16:4–5, 22). He makes no further attempt to justify his position or Aaron's.

Leadership Lesson: **Great burdens can be taken to a great God.**

If your burden seems too great, take it to God. If you face significant opposition, take it to God. If you aren't able to carry the weight, God will provide helpers. He has promised not to lay on us what we cannot bear without his help. Don't react to opposition by offering your own vindication. Rather, seek God's face and trust him to vindicate.

___

When he finally stands up again, Moses reminds the malcontents that their own Levite position has been assigned by God. The God of Israel has separated them from the congregation of Israel to bring them near to himself. There is, therefore, no cause for jealousy. Their anger, Moses reminds them, is really directed against God.

Then Moses proposes a test. Moses tells Korah and his followers to take fire in their censers and stand before the Lord. The censers are bronze trays that contain fire. They are to take censers, the ordinary instruments of the priesthood, and present themselves before the Lord at the door of the tent of meeting. It will be then for God to choose who is holy and who should come near. Moses tells the people who want to take over the priesthood to go ahead and see what happens. He points out that God will judge them.

___

Leadership Lesson: In leadership, it's important to know which criticisms are helpful, which are simply expressions of discontent, and which are precursors to rebellion.

___

The next morning the rebels appear as scheduled at the door of the tent of meeting. The tribes assemble to watch the showdown.

Moses protests his innocence to God. He asks God to reject the offering of the rebels but not to destroy them. God agrees not to destroy the people, but he does destroy the leaders in swift and unexpected judgment. The ground beneath the rebels opens and swallows them, their families, and their possessions. Then fire comes forth and consumes the two hundred fifty men who offered incense before the tabernacle. The vengeance acted out by God is essential to the welfare of the camp. The mutiny must be stamped out without mercy.

As a reminder to the Israelites of the fate that awaits anyone who defies God and his prophet, God directs Moses to gather up the fire pans from among the ashes of dead rebels, beat the pans into flat sheets of metal, and use the sheets to cover the altar. It is to be "a sign to the Israelites" (v. 38).

Even though Moses and Aaron have interceded for the people, the following day the people grumble against Moses and Aaron all over again. When the Israelites stubbornly side with the rebels, a plague breaks out (vv. 41–50). Fourteen thousand, seven hundred die before Moses recognizes what is happening and instructs Aaron to make atonement for the people. Aaron succeeds in stopping the spread of the plague by placing himself "between the living and the dead" (v. 48) and offering incense and atonement for the people.

God offers one last proof to confirm the leadership of Moses and Aaron. In Numbers 17, God orders that twelve rods be gathered, one from each of the twelve tribes, and that the name of the leader of each tribe be inscribed on the rods. On the rod representing the Levites, Aaron's name is inscribed. Each of the twelve rods is placed in the tent of meeting overnight.

The next day, Moses enters the tent of meeting and discovers that, of all the rods bundled there, only the rod of Aaron has budded, bloomed, and produced ripe almonds. Once this miracle is displayed to the Israelites, God orders that Aaron's rod be placed in the ark of the covenant along with the other sacred relics.

Questions for Leadership Development

1. How can leaders tell the difference between criticism and rebellion?

2. What is the best way for a leader to respond to opposition?

TWENTY-SIX

ANGER, PART 2: HITTING ROCKS

*Go ahead and be angry. You do well to be angry—
but don't use your anger as fuel for revenge.
And don't stay angry. Don't go to
bed angry. Don't give the Devil that
kind of foothold in your life.*
Ephesians 4:26–27 (MSG)

Despite all the great leadership traits present in Moses, there is one negative characteristic that appears with some regularity. Gerhard Von Rad says of Moses, "From time to time a wild, fierce anger blazes up in him."[1] In three noteworthy instances, Moses takes out his anger on an Egyptian bully, sacred tablets, and a common rock.

Early on, Moses's anger causes him to murder an Egyptian who is beating one of the Israelites. This fit of uncontrolled passion results in Moses's exile from Egypt. Decades later, when Moses comes down from Mount Sinai and sees the Israelites dancing around and worshiping the golden calf, he shatters the sacred tablets in furious anger. However, it is only Moses's exasperated pounding of a rock that keeps him out of the promised land.

Numbers 20 contains the report of this sin that ultimately keeps Moses from entering Canaan. The lack of drinkable water has once again become a problem for the Israelites. Apparently, the demand on the water supply at Kadesh is so great that the source is depleted, and there breaks out again that spirit of murmuring and complaining that has marked the former generation of Israelites and is now evidenced in their children.

Once again, the Israelites become vocal in their opposition, quarreling with Moses and muttering, "If only we had died when our brothers fell dead before the LORD!" (Numbers 20:3). The Israelites complained about the water at the beginning of their pilgrimage (Exodus 17:2), and now they are doing it again near the end of their journey.

This incident is different from the previous water-from-the-rock narrative, when Moses was told to strike the rock in order to produce water (Exodus 17:6). On that occasion, the Lord instructs Moses to take his rod and some of the elders with him and to strike a certain rock in the sight of the people. When Moses obeys, water gushes from the rock and meets the needs of the people and the livestock. However, this time, the instructions God gives are completely different. This time, Moses is to *speak* to the rock, not *strike* the rock. "Speak to that rock before their eyes and it will pour out its water" (Numbers 20:8).

We don't know why God asks Moses to address the rock rather than hit it, but we can speculate. Perhaps God's intent is to show that he can employ different methods at different times to achieve similar purposes. Or perhaps God wants to demonstrate that, if he can transform a hard rock through just a word, he can transform a hard heart too. Another thought is that God is showing us that a new, more mature generation can be handled in subtler ways—that they don't need the crude impact of a stick. But when Moses *strikes* the rock out of anger, the opportunity for a deeper message is lost. Avivah Gottlieb Zornberg says, "It is not Moses's use of the staff that is the problem, it is his use of *words*. It is his words of anger to the people: 'Listen now, you rebels, shall we produce for you water from this rock?' He is striking the people with his words—wielding words as blunt weapons."[2]

Moses may be the most humble person "on the face of the earth" (Numbers 12:3), but he is not the most patient. He is a great leader who is strong under opposition and who responds in the right way—most of the time. Though Moses has many positive characteristics, anger appears to be his Achilles heel.

Moses disobeys God and speaks to the people instead of to the rock. He speaks in anger and claims partial credit for the miracle, saying, "Listen, you rebels, must *we* bring you water out of this rock?" (20:10, emphasis added). Rather than fully glorify God, he reserves some of the credit for himself.

Leadership Lesson: Leaders have to work intentionally to give all the glory to God.

God *chooses* to work through humans—and often leaders—so it can be very easy for us to think we deserve at least some of the credit. We must develop the practice of giving God all the glory, all the time.

Moses follows the same process that worked at Rephidim. He brings down his wooden staff against the rock, but nothing happens. Moses swings his staff again. At Rephidim, only a single blow was necessary to draw water from the rock. But here at Kadesh, the water flows only on the second blow. Yet Moses has made a terrible mistake, and the consequences of his action will be disastrous (v. 12).

Leadership Lesson: The same problem does not always call for the same solution.

Discerning leadership calls for a wise assessment of all the dynamics involved in determining a solution. If your only tool is a hammer, every problem will look like a nail.

Anger has driven Moses off course, as it has before. This incident occurs on the heels of the death and burial of Moses's sister, Miriam (v. 1). Moses is probably grieving. He is also irritated and indignant, hot with anger and disappointment. Irked by the demands of the people he leads, he angrily strikes the rock.

It is easy to empathize with Moses. He has been leading obstinate, stubborn people for a long time. Even God has grown weary of their incessant insurrection, summing up the character flaws of the unruly Israelites by proclaiming, "You are a stiff-necked people" (Exodus 33:5).

For forty years Moses has been in a difficult place, leading problematic people, encountering one demanding circumstance after another. Each time God has proven himself faithful. Now Moses is an old man and has endured a lot of complaints. Not once do we read of anything encouraging or appreciative being shared with him—only bitter complaints, constant sniping, and continual murmuring.

Hitting a rock a couple of times seems like a little thing, really. But apparently it isn't. It is big enough to crush a dream. Moses's disobedience will disqualify him from entering the promised land. The verdict is rendered immediately: "Because you did not trust in me enough to honor me as holy in the sight of the Israelites, you will not bring this community into the land I give them" (Numbers 20:12).

Leadership Lesson: **When leaders lose their temper, that's often not the only thing they lose.**

In Moses's case, he will lose the opportunity to enter the promised land. Moses's anger keeps him out of Canaan. Leaders can also lose influence and credibility when they let their emotions get the best of them. They can lose momentum. They can lose opportunity.

At face value, the consequence of Moses's anger seems overly harsh. It feels like the punishment does not fit the crime and that "the long, arduous, and faithful ordeal of Moses seems to count for nothing at all."[3] However, as Zornberg says, "One has the sense that God is not judging Moses for a one-time failure. His life of leadership has been characterized by a certain 'hardness' in his relation to the people. While he passionately advocates *for* them to God, he often speaks *to* them with a kind of repressed anger."[4]

Leadership Lesson: **Identifying where you are on an anger scale can help you deescalate before there are damaging results.**

Charles Swindoll says that anger rises along five levels, each step more intense than the last:

1) Irritation: an uneasiness brought about by a mild disturbance. This is usually how anger begins to manifest itself.
2) Indignation, a deeper level of intensity, comes next. Indignation is a reaction to something that seems unfair or unreasonable.
3) Wrath, which never goes unexpressed, is the third level.
4) Uncontrolled anger soon becomes fury, which induces violence.
5) Rage is the fifth and final stage. Rage overcomes a person and inspires acts of brutal violence.[5]

Uncontrolled anger is destructive. It tends to lead to overreaction, causing negative consequences to compound and stack up like a chain-reaction crash. Uncontrolled anger makes it difficult to maintain healthy relationships and often results in others being driven away.

Moses is certainly not the only leader to display anger issues. We live in an age of high stress. It takes maturity and self-control (a fruit of the Spirit) to respond calmly to challenging situations and complaining people. Dealing with anger usually begins with understanding what makes you lose control. Anger is a normal human emotion common to the human experience, and most people, but not all, start learning to control it during childhood.

Leadership Lesson: Learn how to keep your cool when things get hot.

Self-control is closely linked to self-awareness. Are there certain things that trigger your anger? Learn to recognize you are angry before losing control.

Stop, take a deep breath, and find a space to calm yourself. Breathe a prayer asking God to help quiet your spirit and give you wisdom. Lower your anxiety by identifying your underlying feelings and taking charge of yourself. If the action of another angers you, try to empathize with the person. Why are they behaving this way? Learn to express your own deep feelings in a way that is healthy and helpful. It takes a level of maturity to recognize you are angry and to speak in healthy ways rather than lashing out at others. Being able to calmly say, "When you do that, it makes me angry" will earn the respect of others and help you avoid a potential crisis.[6]

Questions for Leadership Development

1. How do you avoid claiming for yourself the glory that belongs to God?

2. What triggers your anger?

3. What strategies do you engage to keep your anger from rising to an unhealthy level?

TWENTY-SEVEN

JOSHUA: NO SUCCESS WITHOUT A SUCCESSOR

A leader's lasting value is
measured by succession.
John Maxwell[1]

Joshua is first mentioned in Exodus 17. He will be named two hundred more times throughout Scripture. In Exodus and Numbers, Joshua plays a significant supporting role as general of the army and Moses's assistant (see Exodus 24:13; 33:11; Joshua 1:1). The son of Nun of the tribe of Ephraim, Joshua was born in Egypt and first named *Hoshea*, which means "salvation." Later, Moses changes his name to *Joshua,* which means "Jehovah is salvation"—the Hebrew equivalent of *Jesus* (see Numbers 13:8, 16; Matthew 1:21 and footnote).

Joshua knew the rigors of Egyptian slavery and must have an aptitude for military leadership because Moses names him general of the army when the Amalekites attack the Israelites at Rephidim. The attack is unprovoked and ruthless enough that the brutality of the Amalekites will be ingrained in the memory of Israel. This is the first military encounter for the recently freed slaves, and it will not be the last.

Joshua only has one day to rally the army and get them ready for the attack, but he does it. The day of the battle, Moses goes up to the top of a hill and raises his hands. As long as his hands are up, the Israelites prevail. Whenever his hands drop from fatigue, the Amalekites gain the advantage. To ensure that his hands remain lifted, Aaron and Hur hold Moses's hands up until sunset, bringing total victory to the Israelites. Warren Wiersbe says, "Israel's great victory over Amalek involved three elements: the power of God in heaven, the skill of Joshua and the army on the battlefield, and the intercession of Moses, Aaron, and Hur on the top of the hill."[2]

Leadership Lesson: You may not always step into leadership during a serene season.

In Joshua's case, he is thrust into leadership at a stressful and critical moment. Leaders often find themselves in positions of great responsibility with little notice, although they may have had a lifetime of preparation. If you suddenly find yourself in a critical leadership situation, you are blessed to have on your side the power of God and the intercession of others.

Joshua accompanies Moses up Mount Sinai (but not into the presence of God) when Moses receives the Ten Commandments. He also accompanies Moses back down the mountain when they hear the sounds of the debauchery associated with the golden calf, which Joshua initially misidentifies as the sound of battle.

Joshua is also one of the twelve spies who explore the promised land, and one of only two (the other being Caleb) who remain faithful and bring a positive report. As a result of their faithfulness, both Joshua and Caleb will enter the promised land.

During the journey through the wilderness, Joshua continues to serve as Moses's aide. He often lingers in the tent of meeting after Moses leaves it (see Exodus 33:11). He has a front-row seat to Moses's leadership—his challenges, successes, and disappointments. There could be no better preparation for leadership than apprenticing Moses.

Toward the end of Moses's forty years in the wilderness, he asks God to appoint a leader to replace him, and Joshua is named that successor (Deuteronomy 31:14). Moses is instructed to lay his hands on Joshua—"a man in whom is the spirit of leadership" (Numbers 27:18)—commission him, and give him authority.

Leadership Lesson: There is no success without a successor.[3]

All great leaders must eventually be replaced, and the most significant contribution many leaders make is preparing the next leader.

The words Moses speaks to Joshua in Deuteronomy 31:7–8 are beautiful and affirming: "Be strong and courageous, for you must go with this people into the land that the LORD swore to their ancestors to give them, and you must divide it among them as their inheritance. The LORD himself goes before you and will be with you; he will never leave you nor forsake you. Do not be afraid; do not be discouraged."

Leadership Lesson: Courage is an indispensable quality of leadership.

Leaders will gain courage from the Bible, prayer, and the encouraging words of others. God commands Joshua four times to be "strong and courageous." Joshua himself will repeat the same words of affirmation to the Israelites in Joshua 10:25. God gives Joshua the recipe for leadership success in Joshua 1. He instructs Joshua to obey the laws of God, to meditate on them continuously, to be strong and courageous, and to reject discouragement (vv. 7–9).

Something of the spirit of Moses has been passed on to Joshua. Joshua has been Moses's understudy in the desert for forty years. He has close knowledge of Moses's leadership and a deep sense of institutional memory. Mentored by Moses since his youth, Joshua has been faithful to his leadership opportunities up to this point. Fortified with the blessing of his predecessor, Joshua is ready for this leadership challenge.

Leadership Lesson: New leaders will have different gifts from past leaders.

New leaders are never exactly like their predecessors, and most are *very* different. Moses is a bold leader, willing to stand before Pharaoh and say, "Let my people go." Joshua is faithful but more of a soldier. He serves brilliantly as a field general, but he does not personally perform miracles like Moses. Yet Joshua is the leader God has chosen for this chapter in the history of Israel. Charles Swindoll says, "When a strong leader appoints his own successor, he usually appoints someone very much like himself. Yet it is frequently God's plan to appoint a different kind of [leader] to begin a whole new dimension that would otherwise remain undeveloped."[4]

After Moses's death, Joshua will lead the nation across the Jordan and into the promised land. He dies at the age of 110.

Leadership Lesson: Once a leader has a clear sense of direction, it is time for action.

When Joshua receives instructions from the Lord, he does not hesitate, delay, or postpone. Joshua immediately announces the plan to enter the promised land. The ability to take decisive action in a timely manner is a characteristic of good leadership.

Questions for Leadership Development

1. What did you learn from the succession that occurred when you were given your present leadership responsibility?

2. Who in your sphere of influence might God want you to prepare for future leadership?

3. As a leader, how do you discern a clear sense of direction?

— TWENTY-EIGHT —

MOUNT NEBO: WHEN LEADERS SAY FAREWELL

*I am now a hundred and twenty years old
and I am no longer able to lead you.
The LORD has said to me,
"You shall not cross the Jordan."*
Deuteronomy 31:2

I like how Stephen Green describes our place in God's bigger story: "One lifetime is too short to complete the mission of God."[1] God's story is not limited to one or even two generations. We are invited to engage the narrative, but we will not outlive the narrative. God's story is not limited to our lifetime. It was being written before we were born and will continue to be written after we are gone. The story of God extends beyond the lifetime of any individual, even Moses.

God tells Moses that he can go up Mount Nebo and view Canaan—the land of promise—before he is gathered to his fathers (Deuteronomy 32:48–52). Moses is terribly disappointed at being forbidden to enter the promised land. He has been in the desert for eighty years, and was on the very border of the promised land thirty-eight years earlier.

Famous business leader Max De Pree says, "The first responsibility of a leader is to define reality. The last is to say thank you. In between the two, the leader must become a servant and a debtor."[2] While "thank you" is not the last thing Moses says, he does say "bless you." But before he says that, he has a few more things on his mind that he wants to share.

In Deuteronomy 3:23–27, Moses pleads with the Lord that he be allowed to enter the promised land. God sternly cuts him short. "That is enough," God says. "Do not speak to me anymore about this matter" (v. 26). And, though Moses is forbidden from speaking to God about it, he is not forbidden to speak to the people.

If Moses regrets striking the rock, he doesn't say so. What he does say is that he regrets not making it to the promised land. Up to this point, Moses has only shared his disappointment with God. Now, he tells the people that he is disappointed not only with God's response but also with Israel's apparent indifference. He shows surprising candor in reproaching the people for abandoning him in his hour of need. "But because of you the LORD was angry with me and would not listen to me" (v. 26). His words are full of disappointment, sadness, anger, and reproach.

When God says no, what do you do? Do you let the matter drop, or do you take your case to the people? Moses chooses the latter. He is forbidden to make the request of God again, but he hopes the people will take up his cause. Moses hints to the people that as he has prayed for them and changed God's mind, so perhaps they could pray for him and change God's mind. But they do not get it. He does not ask explicitly, and Israel does not pray for him. Without their prayer—for perhaps they could have changed God's mind—it is not to be. They are either unable or unwilling to grasp the opportunity. They will not intercede for Moses.

Leadership Lesson: All leaders need intercessors.

Nevertheless, it can be difficult for leaders to ask someone to intercede for them. This illustrates the loneliness of leadership. Sometimes leaders feel that if they have to ask those they serve for intercession, it really isn't intercession. Leaders desire the people they serve to be sensitive, engaged, and aware enough to recognize what is needed. (And sometimes people know even better than a leader what is needed.) However, if intercession is not offered, it is worth prompting them to intercede.

How many leaders are disappointed by the insensitivity of the people they lead? How many leaders are emotionally wounded because the people they served did not get the hints, the inner cries, the unspoken desire, or the silent pleas for prayer? Moses is not asking for a golden parachute. What he longs for is the intercession of the people.

When Moses needs intercession, the only people who ever held up his hands are gone. If Aaron and Hur were still around, they may recognize Moses's veiled cries for help. But Aaron and Hur have already died in the wilderness.

Avivah Gottlieb Zornberg says, "Moses reminded them of every plea that he had made on their behalf, because he thought that they would pray on his behalf that he should enter the land with them . . . he gave them the opportunity [opened an opening for them] to pray for him, but they did not understand him."[3]

Forty years of their complaints, mutinies, and griping. Forty years of manna. Forty years without a sabbatical or a vacation. Forty years later, at the edge of Canaan, if God had again said, "I'm going to destroy them and start over with only you," one wonders how Moses might respond. Moses did not have a bucket *list*. Moses had one bucket item: enter the promised land.

But Moses is forbidden to enter the promised land or mention it to God again. However, he is not forbidden to tell the people his greatest disappointment, so he tells them in Deuteronomy 3:23–26. And then he tells them again in Deuteronomy 4:21–22.

Moses wants the people to intercede for him. When it becomes apparent that there will be no intercession, no changing God's mind, no setting foot in Canaan, Moses resolves to end well. Moses's farewell address takes place as the Israelites are camped on the plains of Moab, where Moses will remind Israel of the covenants they have made with God, name and consecrate his successor, and bless Israel.

In Deuteronomy 33, the final act of Moses is to bless the children of Israel. This farewell act is a beautiful, concluding act of leadership. Moses bestows a blessing, one tribe at a time, just as Jacob did on his deathbed in Egypt so many years before. Moses's blessing is a gift of final petition that God might increase the fruitfulness of Israel. Moses's very last words are words of blessing.

Leadership Lesson: **The best, final act of leadership may be to bless those you have served.**

Leaders need to bless future generations, and especially the leaders who will follow them. Stephen Green says, "Blessing is an act of compassionate imagination."[4] Leaders have the opportunity to speak a creative, life-giving word of compassionate imagination into the lives of the next generation.

Leaders should endeavor to make all their last words—the last words of their conversation, the last words of their day, the last words before transition, the last words before death—words of blessing.

A solitary figure ascends Mount Nebo, climbing all the way to the 4,500-foot peak of Pisgah. It is an amazing feat for a 120-year-old man to scale a mountain of that height. Moses does not die the death of a feeble, old man. Rather, he is still full of vitality. He dies not because his strength is gone but because his mission is finished.

From the summit of Mount Nebo, Moses is allowed one look at the promised land (Deuteronomy 3:27; 32:49–50). From the top of Nebo, he sees the vista of Canaan and the land for which he has longed.

Scripture tells us that Moses is 120 years old when he dies, and his "eyes were not weak nor his strength gone" (34:7). Every leader wants to go out on top, and Moses certainly does. The death of Moses is recorded in Deuteronomy 34:5–6. God himself buries his servant. Charles Swindoll observes that "Moses is the only person in the Bible God personally buried."[5] There has never been a more private graveside service.

We are told that the Israelites grieve Moses for thirty days (v. 8). They then set their sights on the promised land. Moses's grave remains unmarked, unvisited, and known only to God.

The final evaluation of Moses and his leadership is recorded in Deuteronomy 34:10–12: "Since then, no prophet has risen in Israel like Moses, whom the LORD knew face to face, who did all those signs and wonders the LORD sent him to do in Egypt—to Pharaoh and to all his officials and to his whole land. For no one has ever shown the mighty power or performed the awesome deeds that Moses did in the sight of all Israel."

Of course, Moses *will* finally make it to the promised land. When he does, he is, characteristically, at the top of a mountain. And he is, uncharacteristically, not alone (see Matthew 17:1–8; Mark 9:2–7; Luke 9:28–36).

Questions for Leadership Development

1. How do you respond when God says no to your request?

2. How does a leader cultivate intercessors?

3. Why are a leader's last words important?

NOTES

Introduction

1. Doris Kearns Goodwin, *Leadership: In Turbulent Times* (New York: Simon & Schuster, 2018), 97.

2. Goodwin, *Leadership*, 274.

3. Charles Swindoll, *Moses: A Man of Selfless Dedication* (Nashville: Thomas Nelson, 1999), 20.

Chapter 2: Pharaoh, Part 1

1. I am indebted to Greg Mason for this insight.

Chapter 3: Shiphrah and Puah

1. Martin Luther King, Jr., *The Autobiography of Martin Luther King, Jr.* (New York: Warner Books, Inc., 1998), 13.

2. Warren W. Wiersbe, *Be Delivered: Finding Freedom by Following God* (Colorado Springs: Chariot Victor Publishing, 1998), 191.

3. Wiersbe, *Be Delivered*, 192.

4. H. Junia Pokrifka, *Exodus: A Commentary in the Wesleyan Tradition*, New Beacon Bible Commentary (Kansas City, MO: The Foundry Publishing, 2018), 56.

Chapter 4: Jochebed

1. Peter Enns, *Exodus: The NIV Application Commentary* (Grand Rapids: Zondervan Publishing House, 2000), 62.

2. Pokrifka, *Exodus*, 61.

Chapter 5: Anger, Part 1

1. Sir Arthur Conan Doyle, *The Adventures of Sherlock Holmes* (New York: Oxford University Press, 1998), 202.

2. F. B. Meyer, *Moses: Servant of God* (New Kensington, PA: Whitaker House, 2014), 32.

3. Swindoll, *Moses*, 59.

4. James Montgomery Boice, *The Life of Moses: God's First Deliverer of Israel* (Phillipsburg, NJ: P & R Publishing, 2018), 47.

5. Swindoll, *Moses*, 55-56.

Chapter 6: Midian

1. M. Craig Barnes, *The Pastor as Minor Poet* (Grand Rapids: Eerdmans, 2008), 48.
2. Wiersbe, *Be Delivered*, 16.
3. Jonathan Kirsch, *Moses: A Life* (New York: Random House, 1998), 105.
4. Wiersbe, *Be Delivered*, 16.
5. David Brooks, "The Moral Peril of Meritocracy," *The New York Times* (April 6, 2019), https://www.nytimes.com/2019/04/06/opinion/sunday/moral-revolution-david-brooks.html.
6. I am indebted to Scott Estep for this insight.

Chapter 7: The Burning Bush, Part 1

1. Goodwin, *Leadership*, xiii.
2. Enns, *Exodus*, 98.
3. Pokrifka, *Exodus*, 155.

Chapter 8: The Burning Bush, Part 2

1. Gerhard Von Rad, *Moses*, 2nd ed., trans. by Stephen Neill, ed. by K. C. Hanson (Eugene, OR: Cascade Books, 2011), 59.
2. Pokrifka, *Exodus*, 74.
3. Goodwin, *Leadership*, 149.
4. Von Rad, *Moses*, 53.
5. Von Rad, *Moses*, 18-19.
6. Von Rad, *Moses*, 21.
7. Enns, *Exodus*, 124.
8. Enns, *Exodus*, 110.
9. Enns, *Exodus*, 111.
10. Pokrifka, *Exodus*, 80. See also Avivah Gottlieb Zornberg, *Moses: A Human Life* (New Haven, CT: Yale University Press, 2016), 153.
11. Zornberg, *Moses*, 22.
12. Zornberg, *Moses*, 52-53.
13. Zornberg, *Moses*, 53.
14. Enns, *Exodus*, 113.

Chapter 9: Pharaoh, Part 2

1. Meyer, *Moses*, 67.
2. Zornberg, *Moses*, 49.
3. Wiersbe, *Be Delivered*, 29.
4. Enns, *Exodus*, 197.

5. Boice, *The Life of Moses*, 74.
6. Pokrifka, *Exodus*, 165.
7. Wiersbe, *Be Delivered*, 31-32.
8. Pokrifka, *Exodus*, 104.

Chapter 10: The Plagues and the Passover

1. John G. Foote, "When I See the Blood," 1892.
2. Boice, *The Life of Moses*, 86.
3. Swindoll, *Moses*, 196.
4. Enns, *Exodus*, 132.
5. Enns, *Exodus*, 239.
6. The Gospel of John introduces a hyssop branch into the story of Jesus's crucifixion, noting that, as Jesus hung on the cross, someone took a sponge, dipped it into sour wine, attached it to a hyssop branch, and lifted the branch to Jesus's lips so he could draw a drink from the sponge. (See John 19:29).
7. Pokrifka, *Exodus*, 151.

Chapter 11: The Exodus

1. William Williams, "Guide Me, O Thou Great Jehovah," 1745.
2. The Bible reports that six hundred thousand Israelites follow Moses (Exodus 12:37), but the head count only includes men.
3. Enns, *Exodus*, 269.

Chapter 12: The Red Sea

1. Henry J. Zelley, "When Israel Out of Bondage Came," 1896.
2. Kirsch, *Moses*, 187.
3. Swindoll, *Moses*, 219.
4. Swindoll, *Moses*, 222.

Chapter 13: Marah

1. This saying is widely attributed to Woodrow Kroll.
2. Wiersbe, *Be Delivered*, 76.
3. Kirsch, *Moses*, 210.
4. The wood is probably a symbol rather than the means of healing, similar to Moses's bronze serpent for the people poisoned by the snakebites in Numbers 21.

Chapter 14: Manna and Quail

1. Williams, "Guide Me, O Thou Great Jehovah." This hymn is full of imagery based on the journey through the desert to the promised land, as described in Numbers and Exodus.
2. Swindoll, *Moses*, 241.

3. Boice, *The Life of Moses*, 120.

4. Stephen G. Green, *Deuteronomy: A Commentary in the Wesleyan Tradition*, New Beacon Bible Commentary (Kansas City, MO: Beacon Hill Press of Kansas City, 2014), 133.

Chapter 15: Amalekites

1. Wayne Kyle, Chris Kyle's father, quoted in Chris Kyle, Scott McEwen, and Jim DeFelice, *American Sniper: The Autobiography of the Most Lethal Sniper in U.S. History* (New York: William Morrow, 2012).

2. Pokrifka, *Exodus*, 196.

3. I am indebted to Scott Estep for this insight.

Chapter 16: Jethro

1. Pokrifka summarizes the explanations in *Exodus*, 64.

2. Midian was a son of Abraham by his second wife, Keturah.

3. Boice, *The Life of Moses*, 49.

4. Meyer, *Moses*, 149.

5. Swindoll, *Moses*, 253.

6. Swindoll, *Moses*, 251.

7. Pokrifka, *Exodus*, 203.

8. Wiersbe, *Be Delivered*, 98.

9. Two excellent resources on delegation are: Kelly Minter, "Moses and the Mutual Benefit of Delegating Responsibility," February 27, 2019, https://lifewayvoices.com/church-ministry-leadership/moses-and-the -mutual-benefit-of-delegating-responsibility/; and Douge Powe, "5 Leadership Insights from Jethro," April 10, 2019, https://www.churchleadership .com/category/leading-ideas/.

Chapter 17: Mount Sinai

1. Wiersbe, *Be Delivered*, 106.

2. Enns, *Exodus*, 339; Pokrifka, *Exodus*, 211.

3. Meyer, *Moses*, 195.

Chapter 18: The Ten Commandments (First Tablet)

1. Harry S. Truman, "Address before the Attorney General's Conference on Law Enforcement Problems," February 15, 1950.

2. The Bible contains three versions of the Decalogue: Exodus 20 (the classic formula); Deuteronomy 5:6–18; and Exodus 34.

3. Pokrifka, *Exodus*, 214.

4. Green, *Deuteronomy*, 96.

5. Terence E. Fretheim, *Exodus*, Interpretation: A Bible Commentary for Teaching and Preaching (Louisville, KY: Presbyterian Publishing Corporation, 2010), 204. Cited in Enns, *Exodus*, 411. Enns also sees in the Ten Commandments a link to creation, stating that the Decalogue helps bring order to chaos in the same way creation brings order to chaos.

6. Enns, *Exodus*, 414.

7. Enns, *Exodus*, 413.

8. Von Rad, *Moses*, 30.

9. Pokrifka, *Exodus*, 218.

10. Pokrifka, *Exodus*, 219.

11. Wiersbe, *Be Delivered*, 109.

12. Enns, *Exodus*, 415.

13. Boice, *The Life of Moses*, 145.

14. Green, *Deuteronomy*, 84.

15. Pokrifka, *Exodus*, 223.

16. Von Rad, *Moses*, 55.

17. Von Rad, *Moses*, 51.

18. Von Rad, *Moses*, 55.

19. Enns, *Exodus*, 419.

20. Pokrifka, *Exodus*, 224.

Chapter 19: The Ten Commandments (Second Tablet)

1. Kirsch, *Moses*, 249.

2. Pokrifka, *Exodus*, 229.

3. Pokrifka, *Exodus*, 230.

4. Enns, *Exodus*, 423.

5. Pokrifka, *Exodus*, 231.

6. Enns, *Exodus*, 423.

7. Green, *Deuteronomy*, 94.

8. Pokrifka, *Exodus*, 238.

Chapter 20: The Golden Calf

1. C. Andrew Doyle, *Vocatio: Imaging a Visible Church* (New York: Church Publishing, 2018), 152.

2. Kirsch, *Moses*, 269.

3. I am indebted to Steve Estep for this insight.

4. Enns, *Exodus*, 588.

5. Pokrifka, *Exodus*, 396.

Chapter 21: The Cleft of the Rock

1. Augustus Toplady, "Rock of Ages," 1763. This incident has been a favorite topic of hymn writers ranging from Toplady's "Rock of Ages" to Fanny Crosby's "He Hideth My Soul" (1890) to Meredith Andrews's "Open Up the Heavens" (2012).

2. Zornberg, *Moses*, 98.

3. Barnes, *The Pastor as Minor Poet*, 53.

Chapter 22: Bezalel and Oholiab

1. Enns, *Exodus*, 521.

2. Wiersbe, *Be Delivered*, 130.

3. Enns, *Exodus*, 546.

4. Enns, *Exodus*, 522.

5. Wiersbe, *Be Delivered*, 129.

6. Pokrifka, *Exodus*, 379.

7. Pokrifka, *Exodus*, 378.

8. Pokrifka, *Exodus*, 379.

9. Pokrifka, *Exodus*, 300.

10. Wiersbe, *Be Delivered*, 134.

11. Meyer, *Moses*, 193.

Chapter 23: The Twelve Spies

1. Meyer, *Moses*, 217.

2. Boice, *The Life of Moses*, 313.

3. Green, *Deuteronomy*, 50.

4. I am indebted to Scott Estep for this insight.

Chapter 24: The Wilderness

1. See Numbers 7:1-9.

2. I am indebted to Steve Estep for this insight.

3. See 1 Samuel 19-23.

4. See Galatians 1:17.

5. Swindoll, *Moses*, 71.

6. Swindoll, *Moses*, 78.

Chapter 26: Anger, Part 2

1. Von Rad, *Moses*, 6.

2. Zornberg, *Moses*, 159.

3. Kirsch, *Moses*, 13.

4. Zornberg, *Moses*, 159.

5. Swindoll, *Moses*, 302-303.

6. Eddie Estep, *Who's Got Your Back? Leadership Lessons from the Life of King David* (Kansas City, MO: Beacon Hill Press of Kansas City, 2014), 79.

Chapter 27: Joshua

1. John C. Maxwell, *The 21 Irrefutable Laws of Leadership: Follow Them and People Will Follow You* (Nashville: Thomas Nelson Publishers, 2007), 257.

2. Wiersbe, *Be Delivered*, 91.

3. Attributed to Peter Drucker in Maxwell, *The 21 Irrefutable Laws of Leadership*, 215.

4. Swindoll, *Moses*, 324.

Chapter 28: Mount Nebo

1. Green, *Deuteronomy*, 298.

2. Max De Pree, *Leadership Is an Art* (New York: Doubleday, 2004), 11.

3. Zornberg, *Moses*, 177.

4. Green, *Deuteronomy*, 302.

5. Swindoll, *Moses*, 346.

ABOUT THE AUTHOR

EDDIE ESTEP has served the Church of the Nazarene as a district superintendent and a pastor. He is a graduate of Mount Vernon Nazarene University, Nazarene Theological Seminary, and Asbury Theological Seminary. Eddie is passionate about cultivating leaders in Kansas City and around the world. He is married to Diane, and they have two sons, Josh (married to Kortney) and Jeff (married to Brittany), and two granddaughters, Ellie Kay and Emery Ann.

Other Titles in the Series

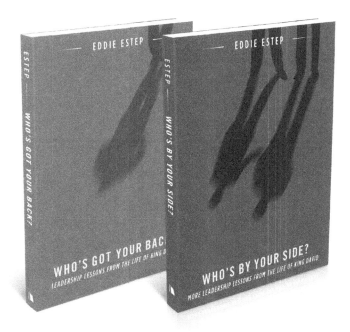

Biblical principles about leadership and relationships are timeless.

In *Who's Got Your Back?* and *Who's By Your Side?*, Eddie Estep examines the leadership lessons we can learn from King David's relationships with family, friends, and foes.

Each book includes questions at the end of each chapter for personal development. These books are perferct for individuals, leadership teams, and small groups desiring to gain wisdom valuable for leaders today, tomorrow, and beyond.

ORDER ONLINE AT THEFOUNDRYPUBLISHING.COM

WHO'S GOT YOUR BACK?
ISBN: 978-0-8341-3361-7
Also available as an ebook

WHO'S BY YOUR SIDE?
ISBN: 978-0-8341-3550-5
Also available as an ebook